# Keys to the Growth of Neighborhood Development Organizations

Neil S. Mayer
with
Jennifer L. Blake

*An Urban Institute Paper*

THE URBAN INSTITUTE PRESS · WASHINGTON, D.C.

LC 81-51756
ISBN 87766-299-1
**Please refer to URI 32600 when ordering**

Manufactured in the United States of America

This volume was printed by The John D. Lucas Printing Company
from type set by Mid-Atlantic Photo Composition

A/81/1500

THE URBAN INSTITUTE is a nonprofit policy research and educational organization established in Washington, D.C. in 1968. Its staff investigates interrelated social and economic problems of urban communities, and government policies affecting those communities and the people who live in them. The Institute disseminates significant findings of such research through the active publications program of its Press. The Institute has two goals for work in each of its research areas: to help shape thinking about societal problems and efforts to solve them, and to improve government decisions and performance by providing better information and analytic tools.

Through work that ranges from broad conceptual studies to administrative and technical assistance, Institute researchers contribute to the stock of knowledge available to public officials and to private individuals and groups concerned with formulating and implementing more efficient and effective government policy.

The research on which this paper was based was supported by funds from U.S. Dept. of Housing and Urban Development.

# CONTENTS

# FOREWORD

The study which follows provides provocative insights into one of the most significant phenomena in community development during the past 15 years—the growth, in numbers, diversity, and effectiveness of neighborhood-based organizations undertaking a broad range of physical development activities. These organizations—called neighborhood development organizations (NDOs) or community development corporations—typically operate in socioeconomic environments which stubbornly defy most forms of revitalization. And in many cities and rural areas, these organizations have coalesced around sets of issues generated by the neglect of their community by the major private and public institutions in the city or area.

The study defines certain key characteristics of neighborhood development organizations and relates these characteristics to NDOs' capability to undertake successfully a diversity of community development activities, such as housing rehabilitation or economic development. The research was funded by the U.S. Department of Housing and Urban Development as part of its continuing research agenda into the forces of revitalization in American cities. Study findings have subsequently provided useful guidelines to the department in the course of initiating its program of support for 125 neighborhood development organizations through the Neighborhood Self-Help Development program. And they should prove useful to any institution, public or private, that is interested in understanding the most effective ways to provide support to neighborhood development organizations.

The study undertakes to answer four basic questions:

1. What organizational characteristics are essential to the success of specific community development projects undertaken by NDOs?

2. What are the best ways to describe and categorize different levels of capability among NDOs?

3. How best can NDOs be supported—with both financial and technical assistance—at various stages of development, in order to undertake community development activities successfully?

4. What are the best measures for gauging the effectiveness of NDOs in using various types of support to undertake community development?

The study involved extensive literature search and interviews with a number of recognized experts, but relies principally upon intensive site visits to 12 neighborhood development organizations throughout the U.S. Chapter 2 describes the key characteristics of the NDOs and their community environment and indicates how certain key characteristics mold organizational capability to undertake community development. Chapter 3 traces the stages of NDO development and growth. Chapter 4 assesses the critical role of financial and technical assistance, particularly at milestones in the development

vii

of organizational capability. Chapter 5 attempts to develop measures of NDO performance that would be useful in future decisions regarding possible support.

The study constitutes an unprecedented attempt to understand the factors that guide success—or contribute to failure—for neighborhood development organizations operating in dynamic environmental circumstances over which they have little or no control. As these organizations continue to contribute in many ways to local community development, such understanding will be essential to the continuing development of public and private policies which can assure successful revitalization.

David B. Carlson
Director
Neighborhoods and Communities Program

# ACKNOWLEDGMENTS

Many people made significant contributions to this research. Karen Kollias, Joe McNeely, Joel Friedman, and Howard Sumka of the U.S. Department of Housing and Urban Development provided valuable advice and support throughout the study.

Ms. Kollias and additional HUD staff members, Alice Shabecoff and Terry Simonette, were particularly helpful in giving the researchers access to HUD materials on specific neighborhood development organizations. These and other members of the Office of Neighborhood Development staff gave helpful feedback on written materials and oral presentations.

The perceptions of numerous funding sources' representatives, technical assistance providers, and researchers familiar with neighborhood development organizations were very useful in designing the study's interview strategy and shaping its analysis. Special thanks are due the staffs, boards of directors, and associates of the 12 neighborhood development organizations who spent long hours sharing their experiences with us. These experiences combine to form the base of information for this research.

Andrew Mott of the Center for Community Change reviewed a draft of this report at HUD's request and contributed many valuable comments.

At The Urban Institute, David Carlson, Harvey Garn, and Mort Isler offered helpful guidance at several stages of work. Robert Rosenbloom contributed greatly to study design while a visiting scholar at the Institute and performed 1 of the 12 case studies after returning to his teaching position at Mt. Holyoke College. Christine Hodge, Joan Sanders, and Mary Garcia efficiently typed and produced the paper.

# I. INTRODUCTION

## BACKGROUND AND OBJECTIVES

In recent years, neighborhood organizations have played a growing role in generating revitalization projects in their communities. These organizations have worked to build and renovate housing, create jobs and businesses, provide commercial goods and services, train workers, and conserve energy. Particularly in seriously troubled neighborhoods, but in many others as well, nonprofit citizen organizations have stepped in to carry out community development activities[1] that traditional private and public actors are unwilling or unable to conduct.

The current scale and scope of neighborhood organizations' work in community development is quite substantial. We shall limit our attention to Neighborhood Development Organizations (NDOs): community-based organizations that undertake the types of housing, economic development, and energy projects listed above rather than playing advocacy or social service roles alone. Hundreds of neighborhood organizations now fall within this definition. A recent study identified over 500 NDOs from lists provided by HUD's Office of Neighborhood Development.[2] More than 700 organizations responded to a HUD request for proposals for NDOs to receive assistance for revitalization project work.[3] The New World Foundation uncovered some 30 NDOs in Philadelphia alone in a case study of that city, as part of a broader analysis of thousands of self-help organizations of various kinds.[4]

NDOs have undertaken a broad range of projects. For example, in the housing field alone, various organizations have concentrated on rehabilitating houses for owner or rental occupancy, encouraging continuing maintenance by existing owners, managing multifamily housing, converting buildings to cooperative ownership, constructing new rental and owner-occupied housing for different populations, weatherizing homes, renovating abandoned housing, and reusing formerly nonresidential structures for housing purposes. Surveys of NDO activity have identified nearly 100 types of community development projects across the spectrum of housing, economic and commercial development, community facilities, job training, and environ-

---

1. We shall use the words "community development," "development," and "neighborhood revitalization" interchangeably to designate the activities listed in this paragraph.

2. The Support Center, "Financial Management Needs Assessment among Neighborhood Development Organizations," Washington, D. C., January 1980.

3. Some of these turned out not to be functioning NDOs, however.

4. The New World Foundation, "Working Papers: Project on Recognition for Initiatives for Community Self-Help," Draft Report, New York City, January 1980.

mental and energy work.[5] And even those lists largely neglect, for example, the variety of business enterprises in which NDOs have become involved.

Furthermore, NDOs are taking on projects of substantial individual scale. For example, a series of 70 NDO projects supported by a new federal program averaged nearly 2 million dollars in expected value of direct results alone, promising to leverage 16 total dollars for each dollar of grant.[6] And some NDOs have grown to very substantial cumulative levels of activity in their individual communities. Among the larger organizations, we find annual budgets in the millions of dollars; employees numbering in the hundreds (internal NDO staff and project workers together); and activities such as managing, maintaining, and/or rehabilitating 1500 apartments under an array of government programs and private contracts.

The resources available to assist NDOs in their work and to implement their projects have been limited and sporadic. Money for general support, planning, and specific project or program efforts; technical assistance of many skill types; in-kind goods and services (e.g., free office space or loaned staff); training sessions and information packets; and recognition, publicity, and legitimation all have been provided by outside actors. Sources of assistance have included various levels of government, foundations, churches, private businesses, labor unions, individuals, and intermediary technical groups. Still, a recent study of aid to NDOs and other self-help organizations concluded

> Our major finding is that while there exists a fascinating variety of forms and sources of recognition and support from a broad spectrum of sources, the scope of assistance does not begin to meet the opportunities and requirements of the self-help world.[7]

At the same time, NDOs differ greatly in their experience and capabilities to carry out their work, with or without additional aid. While the levels or stages of NDO capacity-development are complex to describe, they undoubtedly have powerful impacts, both on the scale and types of activities that NDOs can successfully conduct and on the kinds of assistance that various organizations need and can use effectively.

Given the very limited amount of aid available, it is difficult but extremely important to match outside assistance to NDOs' needs and abilities.

In our research, we examine just how NDOs become successful in com-

---

5. The New World Foundation, Appendix B and *People Building Neighborhoods*, Vol. II (Case Studies), Final Report of the National Commission on Neighborhoods, Washington, D. C., 1979.

6. These grants are the first round of awards under HUD's Neighborhood Self-Help Development program.

7. New World Foundation, *People Building Neighborhoods*, p. II-1.

munity development project work. A principal purpose of the study is to help institutions that assist NDOs in such projects to structure and allocate aid effectively. We also hope to provide information useful to NDOs' own leaders in building their organizations' project capabilities and records of successful project development.

More particularly, we want to answer four related questions:

1. What specific organizational characteristics are essential to NDOs' success in carrying out community development projects?[8]

2. How can NDOs' differing levels of capacity to carry out such projects best be categorized and described?

3. What forms of technical and financial assistance are appropriate for NDOs at various stages of growth, both to help them carry out projects and to increase their capacity to do such work in the future?

4. How can NDOs' effectiveness in carrying out projects and using assistance be measured?

Answering the first two questions is necessary to any systematic effort to support NDO development. The building of project competence and success—whether undertaken by an NDO alone or with sources of outside aid—must be shaped by understanding (1) the capabilities that are most important for an NDO to develop and (2) an organization's current status in developing them. Recognizing what assistance is most valuable under various conditions (question 3) contributes directly to outsiders' ability to aid NDO growth. And properly measuring NDOs' project accomplishments and use of assistance (question 4) provides feedback that can help direct future aid.[9] Careful answers to the four questions can help guide support for the growth of NDOs' project activities and of their skills and capabilities.

To meet our study objectives we first reviewed existing literature on NDOs and interviewed recognized experts in NDO activity and development. Using that groundwork to form study hypotheses, we then visited 12 NDO sites where we talked to people working directly within, or along with, the NDOs themselves. Their views and the inferences we drew from observing NDO characteristics and successes or failures form the basis for

---

8. Since this research does not involve evaluation of the performance of individual projects, success is defined broadly as development and implementation of specific projects yielding their intended outputs, within reasonable costs and time periods given the community environment, and consistent with important community needs.

9. The four study questions are linked not only by their shared purpose but also by the logical dependence of answers to one on answers to others. Those linkages will be discussed in later sections of this paper.

our conclusions about how NDOs grow. (See Appendix A for further information about study methods.)

## FINDINGS AND CONCLUSIONS

The following pages summarize our findings concerning the four key study issues. We describe the characteristics an NDO needs in order to succeed in community development work. We discuss the stages through which important NDO capabilities develop and the ways funding and technical assistance can best serve NDOs. We then indicate how NDO performance can best be measured. In addition, we outline some useful directions for further research.

### Key Characteristics for Success

The factors we found of major influence in successful NDO community development work can be divided into three groups: characteristics internal to an organization—its staffing, management, and structure; an NDO's relations with its community and with other actors in the private and public sector; and the economic, social, and political environment in which an organization operates.

The nine internal characteristics that helped determine NDO project capability include

- Leadership by an effective executive director
- Paid, full-time staff with development expertise
- Control of work levels for key staff
- Doing homework[10]
- Careful, flexible planning
- Board/staff relations: defined roles and shared objectives
- Parent organization control over the development or for-profit spin off
- Legal status as a nonprofit corporation
- Successful track record

Few would dispute that these internal characteristics somehow matter. Chapter 2 specified what aspects of the characteristics are critical and how and why they influence project success.

The key internal characteristics are in general a mixture of factors important to for-profit businesses of similar scale and other features unique to NDOs' nature as community-based and controlled institutions. For example, NDOs' need for in-house technical staff capability is certainly shared with private business. On the other hand, special care and talent are required to build this capability without damaging the community roots that enable

---

10. Homework is defined as properly carrying out the detailed work of grant applications, project design, cost estimation, contract progress, reporting, and similar tasks.

NDOs to succeed under conditions where others fail.[11] Technical expertise is often available only by recruiting outside an NDO's immediate community and paying relatively high salaries. And long time NDO participants are often wary of losing control over policymaking to high-powered staff. Assuring continued community control over policy is à key to preventing internal disputes that often arise over outside hiring. Such assurances are also necessary to retain wide community support. Creating adequate means of assurance requires other internal capabilities including clearly defined board and staff roles and the exercise of special leadership skills by the executive director. Business practices and skills alone do not suffice.

Important aspects of NDO relationships to community and outsiders we identified include the following:

- Roots in the community
- Conflicts and harmony within the community
- Political clout
- Working relationships with local merchants (for applicable projects)
- Working with private project developers
- Outside relations with other private actors
- Sources of continuing administrative and venture funds
- Early aid from private risk-takers
- Access to technical assistance

NDOs operate in neighborhoods whose residents have very limited financial resources and often lack technical training and experience, and where private investment and enterprise and sometimes public action have been in short supply. Obtaining assistance and cooperation from a variety of external sources, combined with community support, is critical to NDO success. The nature and importance of each of the outside relationships just listed are discussed at length in chapter 2.

The difficult environmental conditions NDOs face severely constrain their performance in neighborhood revitalization. This is no surprise, since many of the same environmental factors were important in producing the conditions to which NDOs now react. We categorize and describe the impacts of eight major types of influential conditions in chapter 2:

- Housing and economic market conditions
- Project cost factors
- Housing stock and land use characteristics
- Reluctance by private lenders to lend funds
- Racism and sexism
- Political conservatism
- Timing of political events
- Special situations

11. Both private and public actors.

How NDOs react and adjust to these environmental conditions is extremely important for success. For example, successful NDOs carefully selected projects to correspond to the specific opportunities that housing and economic markets provided or allowed; battled high project costs through such advance-planning means as land-banking; and took full advantage of nonfinancial aid from lenders. These NDO's also used the spectre of "citizen action" and new regulation to encourage lending and pressed administrators of new government programs to make these programs workable for community-based organizations. Since every NDO confronts powerful constraints because of its environment, resourcefulness in recognizing opportunities and minimizing limitations is crucial to project success.

## Stages of Development

How NDOs develop the capacity to undertake revitalization projects is very complex. The process is not divisible into neatly defined stages. Organizations with differing beginnings, neighborhood problems, initial activities, sources of support, and other characteristics take very different paths to maturity.

We can realistically describe NDO growth patterns in two ways. First, NDOs pass through a series of common processes at *some* time in their lives that lead to more successful revitalization project development. Each process involves multiple changes in outlook, knowledge, experience, and a range of specific capabilities. NDOs work through the processes in different sequences, but those that have worked through more processes, more completely, appear notably more adept in project activities. We identified the following significant processes:

- Formally establishing an organization
- Deciding to carry out programs and to create institutions
- Confronting the difficulties of early neighborhood revitalization projects
- Becoming competent in specific project work
- Developing a network of relations with outsiders
- Building a diverse range of projects
- Institutionalizing expanded project competence

While the order of the above processes appears to represent a logical time progression, in fact we observe many variations. Within our set of 12 study NDOs, for example, even two of very similar and substantial longevity and success followed very distinct paths of organizational development.

Second, examining the development of individual key characteristics of capacity, particularly internal capabilities and relations to outsiders listed earlier, helps to describe growth in NDO capability. The characteristics again need not develop in consistent time sequences or particular combinations.

Whatever the order of growth in specific elements of capacity, NDOs with many of these well developed characteristics are relatively advanced in ability to take on projects.

We find that our study site observations also reveal a clear development pattern for a significant subset of key characteristics. These include—among NDO internal characteristics—staff technical expertise, track record, leadership by the executive director, record of "doing homework," and good board/staff relations; and—among relations to outsiders—roots in the community, personal relations with funders, political clout (a less clear growth process), relations with private lenders, and use of technical assistance. Describing the growth process of these characteristics provides numerous implications for actions by both NDOs and external actors to help develop the capabilities. For example, the best personal relationships with funders clearly resulted from NDOs' conscious, deliberate actions to create them, beginning early in organizational development. Since such personal relations are important to funding and hence project success, the strong suggestion is that NDOs must plan and implement strategies to establish continuing personal contacts. NDOs can also benefit substantially from advice by sources of technical assistance, early funders, or other outside actors about the need for contracts, appropriate individuals to contact within complex institutions, and useful means for approaching such individuals.

## Funding Support and Technical Assistance

Obviously NDOs need operating and investment funds from outside sources to carry out significant community development projects and to survive as organizations doing programming more generally. But certain kinds of funding, or their creative use by NDOs, can be especially valuable. Specific funding may affect organizational survival, development of key projects, capacity growth, or ability to raise or productively use other funds. The importance of particular funds may lie in their timing in relation to NDO or project development or in the general level of difficulty in obtaining money for certain purposes. Significant aspects of funding and fund use fall into seven groups:

- Early funding, before an NDO's track record is established
- Sources of flexible and continuing funds
- Important substitutes for flexible funds
- Major increases in funding scale or scope
- Leveraging funds
- Recycling financial resources within the community
- Adequate project funding levels

In general, financial support that allows flexible use of the money, insures NDOs against future cutbacks, meets such special needs as "upfront" funding for planning and early implementation stages of projects, and funds projects adequately is particularly useful to neighborhood organizations. Regrettably, such support is also particularly scarce.

NDOs use their funds more effectively when the activities they undertake are consistent with the level of nonfinancial capacity they have already developed. But there is great temptation for NDOs to seek and accept all available financial support[12] and for funders to assist successful organizations. Both NDOs and funders must work vigilantly to keep overall funding to individual organizations, and the scope of individual projects, in line with NDO capabilities. Sources of support might also want to provide funds specifically for capacity-building efforts, along with the program monies that sometimes strain NDO growth processes.

Many forms of "hands-on" technical assistance prove valuable to NDOs. Important areas of aid include

- Proposal writing
- Project packaging
- Special professional services
- Legal assistance
- Accounting
- Assistance with relations to outsiders, especially funding sources
- Defining board and staff roles and training board members in development
- Organizational structuring and design
- Multipurpose project and organizational counsel

Two broad issues are critical to NDOs' effective use of technical assistance. First NDOs must learn to control the use of outside technical aid. Technical assistance is generally most valuable when an NDO itself has identified, carefully defined, and contracted for specific technical services. NDO staff must have the confidence and knowledge to insist, throughout the contract, that technical assistance providers deliver the specific products promised and operate within the stated guidelines of community goals. NDOs usually learn the importance of such control through their own unsuccessful experiences or the advice of sources of technical assistance with long NDO experience.

Second, many types of technical assistance must be designed for gradual elimination. Successful, mature NDOs perform much or all of their proposal writing, day-to-day project implementation, fund-raising strategizing, and other tasks in-house, although these NDOs may have formerly received a great deal of technical aid. NDOs must structure the delivery of early techni-

---

12. Frequent past shortages of funds, fear of future shortages, and the large scale of neighborhood needs all help create this temptation.

cal assistance to result in the training of their own staffs (and sometimes board membership) and find aid sources who are willing and able to contribute to that process.

## Performance Measures

Measuring the effectiveness of NDOs in carrying out their projects and in using financial, technical, and other aid can play a valuable role in encouraging NDO growth. Such assessment provides feedback on current NDO support efforts that can help to direct future assistance, and it can provide the basis for assuring policymakers that aid to NDOs is a productive use of neighborhood revitalization resources.

Identifying appropriate measures of NDO performance is a difficult and sensitive task. One difficulty is taking into account the full range of impacts that NDO projects may have. Measured project benefits need to include not only primary direct outputs (e.g., houses rehabilitated in a home repair project), but also other direct outputs (e.g., training neighborhood youth to do the repairs) that may be among NDO objectives but not those of other actors undertaking similar projects. The income (and other socioeconomic) distribution of project benefits must also be evaluated, because serving low- and moderate-income and other disadvantaged people is generally a principal NDO goal and can certainly involve added costs and complications. In addition, NDOs' own project efforts and aid from outsiders[13] are often intended to produce not only successful projects but increased NDO capacity for similar future work. The very complex task of measuring improved capability is thus a necessary one.

A second but related type of measurement difficulty is to establish reasonable standards against which to compare NDO performance. One useful standard is the level of direct accomplishments originally proposed by an NDO. That standard is especially relevant because sources of assistance are presumably providing aid on the basis that expected results are worth the requested support. Another potentially useful standard is past performance by other actors in similar projects. But truly equivalent activity may be very difficult to find, given the difficult conditions in which NDOs operate. Adjusting performance measures for differences in many environmental conditions is imprecise at best and often infeasible. It is important not to establish standards so insufficiently comparable that differences between NDO and other actors' project outcomes actually represent differences in project activities and environment rather than differences in true performance.

---

13. Particularly, for example, HUD's Neighborhood Self-Help Development program, whose structure helped to define the approach to performance measurement taken in this paper.

A final major area of complexity in measuring NDO performance is in properly attributing observed neighborhood change to NDO work. Certainly NDO projects will have indirect impacts, as other people take actions in response to the organizations' project activities (e.g. increased home repair by neighbors of NDO-rehabilitated structures). But attempts to separate out reaction to NDO work from the impacts of other events will face the severe difficulties that plague analysis of any neighborhood program intervention. In addition, policymakers are sometimes interested in measuring broad community outcomes, to see whether major changes in neighborhood unemployment, housing deficiency, and other problems have resulted from NDO work. We believe that NDOs, and certainly single NDO projects, cannot be held accountable for outcomes so buffeted by larger external forces. Direct and indirect NDO impacts that correspond to community problems, for example job creation or housing improvement, are much more appropriate measures of NDO performance and use of assistance than are overall community outcomes.

## Further Directions

The findings of our research are based in significant part on one-time visits to each of a sample of 12 NDOs, in addition to interviews with recognized experts in the NDO field. It is clearly desirable to make further observations of NDOs' growth processes and project activities in order to substantiate and extend our results.

Little previous research addresses systematically what characteristics are key to NDO project success, how NDO capacity-growth proceeds, what types of outside assistance are most productive in various circumstances, and how NDO performance can be measured. Examining a larger set of NDO experiences and observing each repeatedly over a period of time would help to assure that our findings provide guidance fully sensitive to NDOs' immense diversity and specifically to their differing patterns of change. Observing some NDOs that have had little or no success would produce lessons about causes of stagnation or demise that observing the relatively successful organizations in our study cannot provide. Measuring the results of NDO work in more detailed, specific terms than our study resources allowed could produce more certain findings about the determinants of both success and failure.

Simultaneously, or in related work, researchers might identify types of projects, associated with types of NDOs and environments, that produce revitalization results worthy of emulation and feasible to reproduce. And attention should be given to means for NDOs to succeed beyond the level of individual projects. If NDOs are ultimately to make significant improvements in the conditions of their neighborhoods, we must learn how the organizations can formulate successful revitalization strategies and select and shape useful projects within them.

NDOs are becoming increasingly significant actors in neighborhood preservation and revitalization. At the same time, the resources they possess and receive for their work will probably remain extremely limited. It is critical that those resources be distributed wisely and that NDOs use them well.

The findings of the research reported here should contribute to our understanding of how to promote NDO growth and success effectively and will, we hope, be useful to NDO supporters and participants for that purpose. Our research confirms many perceptions of direct participants in the activities of NDOs. At the same time, we believe the paper extends that knowledge through careful, empirical documentation; systematic presentation of interrelated observations and the links between them; increased specificity about the nature and impacts of NDOs' key characteristics, growth processes, and use of technical and financial assistance; and the addition of some new insights within each of the study objectives. Improved understanding of NDO development is so important that many further efforts should be made to generate such knowledge and to use it to support NDO work.

## ORGANIZATION OF THE PAPER

The remaining four chapters, corresponding to the four study objectives, provide more detailed discussion of the conclusions just summarized. Chapter 2 identifies characteristics that are key to NDO project success and the ways they are important. Chapter 3 discusses NDO growth processes and levels of development, in terms of broad NDO dynamics and the evolution of individual key capabilities. Chapter 4 examines how funding and technical assistance can best foster NDO progress. And chapter 5 suggests ways to measure how well NDOs perform their work and use help from funders and sources of technical assistance.

# II. KEY CHARACTERISTICS

In this chapter, we describe the principal factors that our research identified as keys to successful NDO revitalization work. Many of these characteristics will not be surprising to experts in NDO development. Their listing supports and summarizes previous thinking on determinants of NDO achievement. Our discussion of such characteristics focuses on expanding understanding of the particular ways in which they prove important to project and broader organizational success.

Other factors that we consider significant have received relatively little past attention in discussions of NDO growth. We concentrate on outlining the basic roles these characteristics play as elements of NDO capability. We also identify several characteristics originally hypothesized to be important that we find not to be key, at least in the experience examined by this study.

We have grouped the key characteristics into three major categories:

- The components of or contributors to capacity that are essentially internal to an NDO
- An NDO's relations with its community (community groups and individuals) and relevant outside actors
- The economic, social, and wider political environment in which an NDO operates

The categories, though distinct as a means of grouping important characteristics, are interrelated. For example, the quality of NDOs' internal capacities affects the likelihood that outside actors will form cooperative relationships with the NDOs. And the harshness of environmental conditions affects how adequate and important particular internal characteristics are.

Our focus in all three categories is on the importance of these characteristics to successful revitalization project work as defined broadly in the introduction. We do indicate that a number of the factors are important for various intermediate purposes, most particularly for raising funds, in addition to contributing directly to project development. But we are interested in the characteristics' impact on fundraising because funding is one necessary, though not sufficient, condition for much project success (raising funds is not an end in itself).

The study also focuses on key factors' contributions to revitalization projects specifically, rather than to broader issues of organizational survival and development, success in other types of program and advocacy efforts, or overall impacts on the community. But significant overlaps are inevitable.

The discussion in this chapter consists primarily of a description of *individual* key characteristics and an analysis of their impacts. We do not attempt to rank the characteristics in order of relative importance for several reasons. First, our observations suggested that the significance of individual characteristics varies both with the conditions facing an NDO and with its level of overall capacity development. Second, specific characteristics are more critical to some aspects of NDO project success than to others (e.g., to fundraising, project development, and implementation) and also are, for that and other reasons, ranked quite differently by different actors. And third, while the study provided an excellent opportunity to learn what characteristics significantly affect NDOs' project success and what their impacts are, the limited sample size and period and precision of observation do not support item-by-item ranking.[1]

We also do not discuss important changes in NDO characteristics over time in this chapter. Dynamic processes by which key characteristics develop, or through which the impacts of given characteristics change, are described in later chapters of this report. We also defer discussing roles that outside assistance may play in those changes.

The three types of characteristics—internal, relations to outsiders, and environmental (plus those that are not key)—are discussed below.

## INTERNAL CHARACTERISTICS

Characteristics of NDOs' staffing, management, structure, and program activity prove important to their success in undertaking development projects. We found that nine internal characteristics are critical:

- Leadership by an effective executive director
- Paid, full-time staff with development expertise
- Control of work levels for key staff
- Doing homework
- Planning
- Board/staff relations: defined roles and shared objectives
- Parent organization control over the development or for-profit spin off
- Legal status as a nonprofit corporation
- Successful track record

We describe each of these characteristics and their impacts below.

### 1. Leadership by an Effective Executive Director

For all NDOs in the study sample, impressive, credible, committed, and confident leaders have been a key to organizations' success in carrying out projects. The qualities are generally embodied in one individual: the executive director.[2]

Leadership style was not an apparent predictor of success. Some leaders were known as highly charismatic, others for their businesslike professionalism, and still others combined these aspects in varying proportions.

---

1. Such ranking may or may not be feasible in a larger scale study of this type.
2. The chief staff executive, also called president, coordinator, and administrator.

But many personal qualities and abilities of these leaders are key to NDO achievement and growth. We discuss some major examples of executive directors' contributions below. Effective leaders, however, played major roles in virtually every facet of NDO work.

Especially for organizations moving from advocacy to program work or into new program areas, executive directors' abilities to identify opportunities, confidence to pursue them, and dedication to their completion are clearly critical to successful growth. Leaders of highly successful organizations constantly saw in the events around them, and in the projects they were already pursuing, the possibilities of additional development. These leaders discussed such opportunities with us during our interviews and more spontaneously with their coworkers in our presence. They also had a good sense of the basic NDO management and organizational requirements necessary to pursue further project work. In particular, they were conscious of the needs and opportunities for building capabilities of their organizations. They carefully identified capacity-building priorities and devised strategies to pursue them.

Directors' specific technical and management skills are less critical in moving projects forward than is an understanding of the role and importance of such skills. Confident leaders proved capable of admitting ignorance. They asked questions when they needed information and brought in other staff and technical assistance to supply specific skills. And outsiders admired that kind of confidence and responded cooperatively to it.

Executive directors also frequently play dominant roles in developing direction—goals and objectives—for NDO work. In our sample organizations, it was generally the executive directors who showed the depth of understanding of their local turf to convert community feelings into a sense of programmatic direction. Articulating that sense of direction and sharing it with frequently changing or growing staffs and boards of directors were important parts of leadership. Executive directors also worked and sometimes fought to assure that new staff and consultants operated according to a community's priorities. They made certain that people with technical skills helped community members and the directors themselves retain control over project work rather than competing with them. Otherwise, some staff members began carrying out projects for the projects' sake rather than to meet community goals, board members grew to mistrust development projects as organizational activities and motivation to work hard diminished for both groups. Executive directors, in addition, often helped mobilize support for NDO goals and increase participation by community residents.

Executive directors' personal effectiveness in convincing outsiders of their own and their organizations' competence and commitment is critical in attracting funds and other project support. In our experience, this was especially true for the many outsiders who, at least initially, had a very limited sense of a given NDO beyond their direct contacts with the executive director. Successful selling could be through rather personalized "hustling" or businesslike "homework," or both. But it consistently depended on directors showing a commitment to the community and at least an understanding of the needs and process, if not always all the expertise, for delivering programmatic results.

### 2. Paid, Full-Time Staff with Development Expertise

Continuing and expanding NDO success in planning and implementing development projects is strongly tied to the full-time availability of at least one skilled and experienced developer/manager with major project responsibility. The individual needs a broad understanding of the development process, knowledge of the specific steps in carrying out projects, actual responsible experience in project planning and implementation, a sense of entrepreneurial opportunity (this ability might be shared with the executive director), and a firm commitment to the community. Such capabilities have been critical to moving specific projects forward efficiently and especially to enabling NDOs to grow rapidly through a series of projects that build upon their strengths and opportunities.

Specifically, *full-time, in-house* staff capability proves a very important attribute.[3] NDOs can and do carry out projects with reasonable success by relying on the skills of outside technical assistance sources. Our observations suggested that this approach is less satisfactory than developing in-house capacity in two ways. First, projects are often delayed or made more costly. Outside assistance is not available as problems arise, and coordinating the work of nonexpert staff with outsiders and effectively carrying out tasks that remain in-house without continuous interaction with the "experts" has proven difficult. Second, part-time outside technical experts apparently cannot perform the role of identifying new project opportunities consistent with communities' needs or initiating appropriate projects. Such work requires time away from specific project tasks and close interaction with an array of staff, board, and community members. Periods of rapid growth in planning and undertaking revitalization projects were highly correlated, for our study NDOs, with the recruitment or successful training of a key staff member with development responsibilities. Some NDOs with impressive goals and plans showed little accomplishment in areas where key development staff positions were vacant.

---

3. The *continuous* involvement of a skilled coventurer *dedicated* specifically to an NDO's efforts may be an effective substitute. Typically, though, coventurers, contractors, or consultants do not compensate for lack of in-house skills. See also "Working with Private Project Developers" in this chapter.

Staff members' specific project experiences have also proven extremely valuable in successfully completing projects. The many details of actually carrying out a project are handled far more smoothly by a person who has handled similar work before. As examples, one organization in our study struggled greatly with the nuts and bolts of rehabilitating houses and another with getting HUD approval for new construction until staff members with past records in those activities were recruited. Once on board, the experienced staff members were able to move the projects forward.

The processes through which these and other aspects of technical expertise are developed in house by an NDO are detailed in chapters 3 and 4 of this report.

### 3. Control of Work Levels for Key Staff

Protecting key staff members, and particularly executive directors, from being continually overloaded with tasks in an element of NDO management important to project successes. Limiting workloads to manageable levels appears significant in producing the careful homework (e.g., proposal development, personal presentations of project ideas) that helps earn funding; in carrying out major projects in a timely way; in avoiding burnout and loss of key project staffers; and in creating opportunities to plan for future development.

The ways overload and control are manifested seem to vary with the experience and scale of an organization. For less project-experienced organizations with modest-sized staffs, one way to control workload has been limiting the number of outside requests or project possibilities to which the organization will respond even in areas of interest. Such limitation allows resources to be directed to developing a visible track record and a project focus. The improved control may be gained for example, by establishing a formal project selection process in place of requests from board members to individual staffers. Learning to estimate realistically the staff resources required for development projects also is a key to reducing overload at early stages.

The management and control aspects of workload problems should not be viewed in isolation, however. Some smaller organizations have funding for so little staff that improved management alone is not an answer. Additional funds are needed to support a core group adequate in size and skills to perform basic NDO functions.

For organizations with more development projects underway and larger staffs, dividing major tasks among a sufficient set of project managers (and growing no faster than managers can be obtained) can be critical. Otherwise, site visits showed, NDOs that depended too heavily on one or two people were in danger of giving inadequate attention to project follow up and detail. The slippage could interrupt their records of successful project development and delivery that provided the credibility with outsiders to fuel rapid expansion. NDOs must also be selective about the sometimes numerous funding opportunities that arise because of past success. This was difficult for organizations which may earlier in their histories have faced continuing fund shortages and become used to pursuing all funding possibilities.

### 4. Doing Homework

For many of the organizations in our study, establishing a substantial record of "doing their homework" was crucial in attracting funding and political support for particular projects. Outside sources of support defined homework to include a number of specific elements. NDOs should be skilled at preparing proposals that follow required forms and formats or that create their own logic when official formats are open-ended; making clear oral presentations to political review and funding bodies; patiently explaining and lobbying for projects on a person-to-person basis; understanding and following step-by-step bureaucratic funding processes; accurately predicting funding needs; correctly assessing and reflecting the priorities of community residents; and being prepared with intelligent questions at meetings about new opportunities for support. Program administrators, elected officials, and lending institutions all repeatedly mentioned homework components.

Good current homework performance helps any given project proposal obtain approval. A clear oral presentation, for example, naturally wins more favor—and both NDO staff and sources of support say significantly more—than an incompetent one. Chapter 3 of our study discusses how a *history* of good homework is also important for future projects.

Homework is more important for organizations heavily funded from local sources, in the experience of study NDOs, because of more frequent and varied direct contacts with funders. Homework is also more important for organizations with less charismatic leadership. These organizations cannot rely as heavily on personal contacts by the executive director for funding. Even for NDOs with charismatic leaders, however, one useful part of growth seems to be recognizing the need and then developing the skills for careful homework.

### 5. Planning

Planning by NDOs takes many forms. Skill and effort in some but not all of these forms were important to project success for our sample NDOs.

The least useful type of planning was a one-time process resulting in a comprehensive, written, long-term plan. Such a plan was apparently rarely specific enough to be linked to continuing NDO concerns and activities, was too abstract to attract attention from a board of directors, and was often supplanted quickly by action plans or specific project opportunities. In addition, these plans sometimes created delays in programming that led supporters to question NDO progress or gave early alerts to competitors who captured desirable land or buildings.

Much more useful was an informal, continuing "planning" process for developing an organizational focus and strategy. Often, that process was largely a series of discussions among key staff and board members producing reasonable consensus on the type of projects to pursue. Resourcefulness—in identifying new opportunities, seeing how to build future work from existing projects, and anticipating and responding to changed environment—was the planning skill necessary to move forward from broad strategy. As a clear example of response to the environment, several of our sample NDOs in neighborhoods showing signs of revitalization are acting in anticipation of displacement problems. They are using land and building-banking to ensure that future housing projects will not later be too expensive for community residents. Another NDO currently suffers the high land and structure costs for its rehabilitation projects that result from neglecting that issue for too long. And the most successful of our sample NDOs have the ability to generate, with careful planning, one project from another. For instance, one used housing management experience to attract a coventured new construction project. In another instance, an NDO negotiated with a potential tenant of the industrial structure the NDO was constructing to hire its new workers from the NDO's manpower-training program.

Narrower, more traditional elements of detailed project planning have also been important to sample NDOs: proposal writing and packaging to attract funding, and budgeting and operations planning to implement projects successfully. The first two types, especially their technical aspects, were successfully purchased as outside consultant services in a number of cases and are probably less essential as "inside" skills than the informal planning just discussed.[4] NDOs seemed to learn budgeting and operations planning by trial and error. Experience taught NDOs first the importance of planning and then the skills to carry it out.

### 6. Board/Staff Relations: Defined Roles and Shared Objectives

A clear, internally agreed-upon definition of the separate roles of board members and staff seemed important to NDOs in our sample—to reduce conflict, smooth internal administration, and increase productive work by the board. In particular, disagreements over powers to hire and fire, usually in the context of a specific individual's case, produced frequent acrimony and sometimes loss of support from important community participants.

---

4. The use and timing of technical assistance for these purposes are discussed in detail in chapter 4.

NDOs handled personnel decisions and disputes far better in cases where they had defined clear lines of authority and appeal.[5]

Some boards of directors acknowledged the separation of detailed staff administrative responsibilities from board policymaking more easily than others. They provided more time and energy to perform such important board functions as selecting project focus and generating community, political, and financial support. Several sample NDOs had worked (or were working) through role definition over extended periods, sometimes with neutral outside help. Care by executive directors and staff to share information aside from and in advance of major decision making was apparently important in helping to build trust among board members, which then helped them to accept more easily their separate roles.

In addition, staff and board members must develop a common conception of what an NDO's role in development should be. Otherwise project selection and planning proceed less smoothly and valuable time and energy is sidetracked to repeated fighting of old battles. Major elements of board/staff agreement have included whether development projects are an important part of the overall agenda, whether the NDO should be an owner or operator or only facilitate projects, and whether profits are a legitimate objective. Executive directors with clear conceptions of these issues and close personal links to both board and staff were effective in helping promote a common vision, as discussed earlier. Some NDOs took pains to educate community board members in the language and techniques of development. That education apparently contributed to the board's sense of confidence and control and made it reach easier to agreement on the role of development.

### 7. Parent Organization Control over the Development or For-Profit Spin Off

Close control by the "parent" nonprofit NDO over any spin off organizations created for specific project purposes is clearly most effective in producing successful projects and organizations. NDOs with controlled spin offs were better able to exploit available resources and opportunities, avoid internal conflicts, and keep project activities in line with community desires and needs. Three quarters of the NDOs we studied either have created spin off bodies or are themselves spin offs from original for-profit organizations. Their experience systematically demonstrates the desirability of effective control by essentially a single board and staff.

Organizations with tightly controlled spin offs were able to create and use them for very specific purposes that further the NDOs' project goals. One NDO, for example, created a for-profit real estate company to convert costs

---

5. In some cases, disagreement over the merits of a case might have been acrimonious even when the process and final responsibility were well defined.

such as sales commissions for NDO real estate transactions into NDO earnings and to be able to pay better salaries to technically skilled staff who can then sell their services back to the parent. Tight control is inherent in such strategies of formally moving funds, activities, and people around to increase project benefits and capabilities. NDOs with looser linkages sometimes ended up in protracted negotiations with their own spin offs to divide roles and coordinate activities. These NDOs could not freely shift resources for strategic purposes because they might lose control over, and again need to negotiate about, their use.

Highly separated spin-off organizations also resulted, among our sample of NDOs, in staff jealousies over salaries and responsibilities; confused perception of organizational relationships by community people and funding sources; and, in one instance, use of spin-off activities to benefit spin-off board members. When an NDO with good community roots and some internal capabilities exists, the clear advantage is to use spin offs as controlled *devices* and not to try to create additional responsible organizations.

### 8. *Legal Status as a Nonprofit Corporation*

Obtaining legal status as a nonprofit corporation is essential at a very early stage in an NDO's life, enabling it to qualify and contract for funding, attract membership and board directors, and participate in community development programs.

Foundations and public funding sources overwhelmingly set forth nonprofit corporate status as a basic requirement for funding. Individual contributors to an NDO are also encouraged by being ensured of tax benefits from their contributions. In contracting, corporate status provides a substantial degree of protection from personal liability for an NDO's board of directors— an item of considerable concern to board members in organizations newly moving into programmatic work. In addition, nonprofit status helps prevent an NDO from becoming a tool for personal financial gain of its leaders—an issue of concern to membership and other community residents.

Every NDO studied had obtained nonprofit corporate status for either the parent organization or for its development spin off. That occurred prior to receiving grants from any governmental agency for development projects, either in response to specific agency request, general requirements, or perceived opportunities. None lost that status, but several noted the importance of avoiding activities that could threaten it, structuring spin-off organizations that could handle ineligible activities, and using legal counsel to avoid errors.

### 9. *Successful Track Record*

A successful track record is a key NDO characteristic quite different from those just discussed. To a significant extent, a good track record is a result produced by other capabilities, both internal capacities already outlined and relations to outsiders discussed below. And a track record also strongly reflects the level of difficulties and opportunities an NDO's environment presents.

At the same time, once a substantial track record of successful projects and programs is established, it proves of great value to NDOs' further development. Perhaps the clearest impact for the NDOs in this study is the effect on their ability to obtain funds. Young NDOs may attract initial funding because of their roots in a community, participants' personal credibility, or political ties (especially funds from foundations and churches). Thereafter, continued funding of all kinds, and particularly expanded grants and contracts from government sources, depends significantly on demonstrated ability to deliver program results.[6] Some fairly young organizations carefully develop this kind of credibility, selecting projects that can show positive results in the relatively short term, or for example, rehabilitating part of a block or building to attract support for completion.

The payoffs can be substantial. Some of the more project-experienced NDOs we visited are now sometimes sought out by government funding sources to accept funds for programs that the agencies want to be successfully implemented. Such NDOs also find their own funding requests widely well received. Such factors as personal ties and political clout still play important roles in funding. But a successful track record is at least a necessary, if not sufficient, condition for success in obtaining money and other needed assistance.[7]

A successful track record also is significant in building grassroots support for NDO activity.[8] Highly visible projects (new or improved housing, for example) helped NDOs gain name recognition and assure people that time and money put into the organization were producing worthwhile results. Social service and housing counseling projects that successfully delivered direct benefits to large numbers of community residents were very helpful in building a base of support for several of our sample NDOs. Those programs were particularly valuable in building track records at early stages of NDO growth, because they could often be delivered far more quickly and widely than housing and economic development projects. For a few organizations

---

6. Our definition of NDO is intended to include only those organizations that do elect to carry out programs. Other neighborhood organizations may receive continued support as advocates and organizers.

7. Track records of activities other than project delivery also can be helpful. NDOs faced with hostile local governments have been able to use their records of successful organized political "actions" or lawsuits (apparently as implicit threats) to pry loose funds and other cooperation.

8. The importance of community roots and support is discussed further under "Relations with the Community and Relevant Outside Actors" in this chapter.

whose extended planning processes had not yet produced program results, the lack of visible services caused some community members to question whether resources would be put to good use.

Successful project experience also is clearly a major element of training good NDO staff—allowing them to learn what work steps are required to achieve project objectives and what patterns of project development will be effective in the future. A good track record contributed to staff recruitment and retention as well. And it seemed to give staff the self-confidence needed to admit difficulties and to seek and use outside technical assistance. We discuss the role of project experience in staff and other capacity development at greater length in chapter 3.

## RELATIONS WITH THE COMMUNITY (GROUPS AND INDIVIDUALS) AND RELEVANT OUTSIDE ACTORS

NDOs' abilities to attract involvement, support, and cooperation from a variety of actors are critical in achieving project success. The aspects of relations to community members and outsiders we find especially important are the following:

- Roots in the community
- Conflicts and harmony within the community
- Personal relations with funding sources
- Political clout
- Working relationship with local merchants (for applicable projects)
- Working with private project developers
- Outside relations with other private actors
- Sources of continuing administrative and venture funds
- Early aid from private risk-takers
- Technical assistance

We discuss each in turn below.

### 1. Roots in the Community

The strength of an NDO's roots and support in its own community, and staff and board commitment to the community, is significant to project success in many ways. Among our sample NDOs, the areas of significant impact included program selection and implementation, staff and volunteer energy for hard work, fundraising, and protection when the organization was in trouble. For NDOs which are coalitions of organizations, member organizations' community roots were equally important.

Often, an NDO's roots and support in the community[9] helped to identify projects of genuine use to the neighborhood, design them to meet resident needs, attract program participants, and successfully implement program activities. For example, one NDO built the links needed to work directly with public housing tenants to specify needed housing quality and security improvements. Another knew from experience with community members of the need to attach extra training and services to its manpower programs, to help trainees travel to work or find childcare. Other NDOs used the personal credibility of staff and board members in their communities to attract hesitant homeowners into housing repair programs. NDOs took advantage of neighborhood support for their organization to protect their buildings from vandalism. Repeatedly, the unique success of NDOs in difficult circumstances seemed built on special sensitivity to and support from community voices.

Staff and board members' commitment to the community is also critical in making them willing to contribute long hours of work at low (or no) pay. Invariably, funds and staffing were so limited that these personal sacrifices were required to meet project goals. NDO staff and directors noted that the feeling of being supported by the community and of working in line with genuine needs of residents was a key—along with their initial sense of commitment—to their willingness to continue work, especially in the fact of recurrent crises and setbacks.

In addition, community support for an NDO—evidenced, for example, at public meetings, in demonstrations, at NDO community congresses, in board and other volunteer participation—is often important in attracting financial aid and technical assistance. Many institutions, especially national foundations and religious groups and some federal government agencies, apparently placed heavy weight on an NDO's history of community participation and control.[10] Finally, genuine neighborhood roots were significant when an NDO's projects went poorly or when accusations were leveled against an organization. NDOs which were trusted and had good networks of contact in their own neighborhoods could use the networks to communicate their explanations and retain credibility and support.

### 2. Conflicts and Harmony within the Community

Several NDOs in our study had fairly long-running disagreements with other actors in the community. These conflicts created difficulties for their

9. In some cases, especially early in NDO development, community roots were not so much those of NDOs themselves as organizations but were the linkages brought by individual board and staff members.

10. At the local government level, community roots seemed more important as an element of electoral political clout, discussed separately in this chapter.

activities generally—not neighborhood revitalization projects more particularly. The predominant cost was in draining energy. Even where the NDO regularly won its series of battles, critical time was expended in extra lobbying, attacking, and defending. In addition, credibility with some funding sources and community residents was sometimes significantly reduced by public conflict. Conflicts were, however, neither impassable obstacles to NDOs' success nor necessarily indicators of mistakes or lack of capabilities of an NDO.

Sources of continuing conflicts included competition with other organizations for "rights" to funding and to projects, disagreements with people who withdrew from NDO activity over such issues as staff hiring and power but remained politically influential, and several other fairly unique elements. Our sample is far too small to conclude how common each might be, especially because many NDOs avoided these conflicts. Some enjoyed a well-defined sharing of responsibilities among neighboring groups, producing a range of advantages.

Conflicts were not always without benefits. In at least two instances, observers and participants thought NDOs had considerably strengthened their general credibility and specific track records by preserving revitalization projects in the face of attack. And some NDOs seemed to have improved their skills of mobilizing support by facing the need to organize in a conflict context.

### 3. Personal Relations with Funding Sources

Good personal relationships with funders (or with third parties who have those ties) are a significant element in NDO fundraising for projects and general support. In a number of instances, particularly early in organizations' lives, relationships established by NDO participants before they joined the organization or outside their NDO work prove useful. Examples in our study included staff or board contacts as former employees of local government, private friendships with long-time bank employees, and past political work with people who have links to local foundations. In addition, people with influence over funding decisions have sometimes participated directly in creating NDOs and then helped provide support.

Many organizations consciously pursue the development of personal relationships as part of a deliberate long-range funding strategy. Executive directors do the bulk of this work—some as a natural outgrowth of their personal style and some by forcing themselves to make contacts they believe are necessary for NDO success. Creating a wide network of such connections is especially important for NDOs with less positive relations with their local government.

### 4. Political Clout

Political clout has significant impact on NDOs' ability to attract and maintain funding, obtain other services from the local government and protect themselves from attack by outsiders. At times it may be direct electoral power. Residents can either replace local elected officials with people friendly to the NDO or cause those in power to see the NDO as a significant voting constituency, thereby ensuring support for NDO projects. In our study, several groups with good track records but limited voting power in their neighborhoods continued to have difficulty in prying loose substantial flexible funds, such as CDBG money, that were instead granted to more powerful constituencies also eligible for them.

Political clout also influences local government administrators in two major ways. Local government agencies supported some NDOs that had political contacts at the national level partly in order to gain information or political support for city projects at the federal level in return. Other NDOs had enough clout with elected officials to change the behavior of otherwise less supportive administrators. This impact can be important in getting prompt processing of permit applications, carrying out building inspections, and other necessary tasks. In addition, NDOs use ties with individual politicians, based on a mixture of clout and personal contact, to keep powerful outside enemies from launching attacks.

However, pinpointing the role of political clout is quite difficult. Particularly at the local government level, we (and our interviewees) found it difficult to distinguish between the roles of electoral clout and a successful track record in obtaining project funds.

### 5. Working Relationship with Local Merchants
### (for applicable projects)

Developing projects that involved private commercial retail and service businesses generally proved more difficult for our sample of NDOs than did developing housing projects. One principal reason was difficulty in attracting the participation of existing merchants in the areas in question, whose active agreement NDOs needed to pursue storefront improvements, joint marketing efforts, or opposition to rent hikes.[11] NDOs often lacked direct previous links with business owners. They had difficulty interesting them in cooperative action. Many merchants doubted that the NDOs could identify programs that both addressed their real problems and were practical to implement.

---

11. While attracting merchant participation is a significant complicating factor in commercial revitalization projects, there are also many largely economic factors that make such projects more difficult than housing projects. Our attention to relations with merchants is not intended to downgrade those economic factors.

The key ingredient to getting active participation appeared to be involving merchants very early in specific projects and in the NDO itself. For example, one NDO's first storefront beautification effort failed when merchants objected to preconceived plans. A second effort—involving early meetings between an architect and each store owner to discuss merchant needs, and between project staff, store tenants, and owners to discuss division of costs—was more successful. Two other NDOs backed away from initial plans to pursue commercial projects after failing to gain active merchant participation. Those NDOs are now seeking other "organizing strategies"—strategies that would establish continuing communication and trust between NDOs and local merchants before tackling traditional business problems.

### 6. *Working with Private Project Developers*

Participation by an experienced private development group jointly with an NDO helps the NDO attract project funding and may help implement a project smoothly. In several instances, the track record of a general contractor or joint venture partner directly substituted for NDO experience[12] in winning project loans or grants from lending institutions or government agencies. This was especially important for organizations new to development work or for more experienced groups that were taking on larger and more sophisticated projects than they had previously developed. The private sector actor also sometimes contributed access to responsible special technical services (architects, engineers), knowledge of the steps in the development process, and genuine skill in carrying out specific project tasks.

For long-term capacity development of NDOs, impacts of these partnerships are more mixed. Some organizations very deliberately seek to develop in-house skills and experience in the process of working with the private sector. In at least one case, where the passage of time allows us to examine the results, the pay off appears substantial. The knowledge gained and credibility obtained from joint development clearly helped make the organization an independent project developer. As this chapter already indicated, however, working with outsiders as a *substitute* for building in-house technical capability usually, though not always, limits NDO growth.

### 7. *Outside Relations with Other Private Actors*

NDOs have difficulty involving the private sector regularly and widely in their work. But several did obtain significant aid for particular projects, besides the specific joint ventures discussed. In various instances, a single individual in the business world (e.g. corporate executive, downtown development interest, or business consultant) was instrumental in attracting pri-

---

12. That is, the NDO's track record was not adequate to secure the funding alone.

vate funding, technical advice, a special insurance pool, a private medical clinic, or a factory or grocery chain to NDO neighborhoods in support of their projects. Particularly in NDOs' relations with the business community, using relations with one outsider to make or improve relations with others has sometimes been more productive than an NDO's direct attempts to make or improve those links. A number of organizations realized the difficulty they have in making business connections and worked carefully to build further linkages through the few good contacts that coincidence or hard work produced.

NDOs find it useful to build new relationships from old ones in areas other than the business sector. Foundations funding NDOs at early stages often provided credible openings to other foundation sources and foundation-linked providers of technical assistance. In several instances, foundations formed a local network that provided information about specific NDOs to its "members," further easing an organization's path to wider foundation aid.

## 8. Source of Continuing Administrative and Venture Funds

Commitments of flexible, continuing outside funds appear to benefit greatly NDOs that manage to garner them. The value and dangers of these funds, and potential substitutes for them, are discussed in detail in chapter 4, along with other key funding assistance issues.

## 9. Early Aid from Private Risk-Takers

Before developing a track record, NDOs need the aid of risk-takers willing to gamble on the neighborhood organizations' potential. This early assistance enables NDOs to build track records in the community and with other funding sources and technical assistance networks. Early assistance from churches or local foundations was the most common example of this aid, proving important to nearly half of the NDOs we studied. Other types of early risk-takers included national private foundations and networks which assisted NDOs located in particularly hostile environments.

The range of assistance is wide. It includes direct funding, technical assistance, volunteer staff, and meeting places for young NDOs with extremely limited resources. Individuals from churches and other institutions associated with NDOs as organizers, other volunteer staff, board members, and project work crews. Participation by locally respected organizations and individuals especially helped NDO organizing efforts, by giving them legitimacy in their communities. Early risk-takers who are respected regionally, or nationally, opened doors to funding and technical assistance networks by legitimizing the NDO to such outsiders. Further discussion of the importance of early risk-taker *funding* is contained in the first part of chapter 4 of this paper.

### 10. Technical Assistance

The availability and effective use of many forms of technical assistance from outside sources is very important to NDO project success and capacity development. The types of technical aid that are most useful—and the circumstances in which they are best used—are given extensive attention in chapter 4.

# ECONOMIC, SOCIAL AND WIDER POLITICAL ENVIRONMENT

The economic, social, and political conditions within which NDOs operate fundamentally affect their ability to carry out successful development projects. Indeed, in many instances NDOs' projects are intended to substitute for private or public sector actions that such external conditions rendered infeasible, ineffective, or neglected.

While every NDO faces difficult environmental conditions, the particular external characteristics, their specific impacts, and means to deal with them do vary widely within our sample. The types of characteristics we found significant are the following:

- Housing and economic market conditions
- Project cost factors
- Housing stock and land use characteristics
- Reluctance by private lenders to lend funds
- Racism and sexism
- Political conservatism
- Timing of political events
- Special situations

Next, we specify the meaning and importance of each and suggest how some NDOs have successfully designed strategies to respond to difficult conditions.

### 1. Housing and Economic Market Conditions

Major aspects of housing and economic market conditions significantly influence the potential success of NDO revitalization projects in much the same way that they affect projects by private entrepreneurs. Unsurprisingly, the impacts are often very profound. After all, in many cases market factors such as declining incomes of neighborhood residents and weakening housing markets played major roles in producing the conditions to which NDOs now react. It is therefore no surprise that the same forces have substantial effects on NDOs' ability to carry out work to change existing conditions.

A general description of the key aspects and their impacts is impossible to make. The type of project an organization undertakes and the size of the area in which it considers projects are among the factors that produce diversity in which market components matter. Below we discuss some of the components that arose commonly for the 12 organizations we visited.

Organizations focusing on housing programs in narrow geographic areas were buffeted by the full spectrum of neighborhood housing market conditions. Several NDOs operated in weak low-income housing markets in which most actual and potential tenants could afford standard housing only if they received deep subsidies. The availability of public funds thus constrained levels of activity; mobilization of significant private owner and lender action was unlikely; and new problem buildings (abandonment, etc.) arose as NDOs dealt with others. Some other NDOs had the advantages of operating in mildly revitalizing private markets, in which private homeowners could afford at least modest repair costs and might expect repair investments to be captured at resale. Their cooperation could be more easily obtained along with, to a limited extent, the participation of lenders. Still other NDOs operated in tight local housing markets under heavy development pressure, producing high purchase costs, competition for sites for construction and rehabilitation, and a need to plan and secure property for projects long in advance to assure control.

In commercial and manufacturing development, geographic focus and metropolitan trends were often key. Some organizations undertook local commercial revitalization in distressed neighborhoods. Those efforts often suffered from limited markets, produced by both the poverty of the local community and the metropolitanwide trends of shopping in suburban shopping centers—though sometimes a good opportunity existed to provide neglected goods and services. NDOs taking a wider geographic view and operating in growing metropolitan areas were sometimes able to take advantage of general metropolitan expansion to develop job and profit-generating activities of their own—for example, building and leasing manufacturing facilities to incoming firms.

### 2. Project Cost Factors

Very simply, some NDOs faced significantly higher direct project costs than others. These included such straightforward items as land costs to housing development organizations in strong real estate markets, fuel costs for housing managers in cold climates, and transportation costs in a rural area with inadequate facilities. The extra costs made certain projects financially infeasible, raised the income level of those who could be served, or forced organizations to scramble for additional funds to couple with basic project funding, as well as simply resulting in higher per unit expenses.[13] Lower

---

13. To the extent that the last is the case, in any evaluation of NDO performance higher costs should be considered in setting appropriate standards for comparisons. See chapter 5.

land and building purchase prices in particular made it far easier for some of our sample NDOs to fund projects and meet project goals.

### 3. Housing Stock and Land Use Characteristics

A variety of characteristics of existing housing and land use patterns affect the difficulty NDOs face in developing certain projects. In our sample, these included such factors as how feasible the original structure of existing substandard housing made rehabilitation, whether the attractiveness of existing housing units and land uses made displacement by upper income people a neighborhood problem, whether vacant land was available for desired construction projects, and whether basic infra-structures (sewer, water) existed to support other development. In a number of these instances, the problems resulted mainly in limiting the options in project selection, including loss of eligibility for federal and local programs, rather than complicating implementation.

### 4. Reluctance By Private Lenders to Lend Funds

For a number of organizations, the growth of program operations was significantly slowed or potentially limited by difficulty in obtaining lending capital from private institutions. Traditional patterns of lending to large-scale, low-risk suburban subdivision development still dominated. Most lenders saw loans to NDOs, or housing rehabilitation and small businesses loans in connection to NDO work, as high cost and risky. Lenders often indicated that such loans might be made sometime in the future, either when collateral and experience might justify them or as limited special favors. Particularly notable was the fact that some lenders who were described by both themselves and NDO staff as friends or cooperators with an NDO nonetheless seemed very reluctant to provide actual loans of their own funds where any risk was present.

In such cases, NDOs were more likely to receive other forms of assistance: use of foreclosed buildings, technical assistance, introductions to other members of the business community, small grant contributions, pass-throughs of lender allocations of public funds such as state or municipal mortgage bond proceeds, or perhaps loans guaranteed by public funds or contracts. In a few instances, agreements had been reached for potential loan funding (either to the NDO or more probably to private citizens in connection with NDO efforts) but no loans had as yet been made.[14] Actual NDO projects were funded overwhelmingly from sources other than private lending.

---

14. The reason seemed to be a mixture of continued reluctance by lenders to approve loans in any individual cases and a shortage of cases to date in recently started programs.

The private lending situation is not unmixed. Several organizations we visited did actually obtain uninsured loans, for operating capital or projects. Personal contacts or major participation by other private venturers seemed to play major roles in such instances.

Interestingly, NDOs cited the incentives of the Community Reinvestment Act and city and state level regulation in several cases in which lenders had agreed to provide or actually provided loans. NDOs' use of these levers and numerous other devices to attract lender participation in their projects are described under "Development of Key Characteristics of Capacity" in chapter 3.

## 5. Racism and Sexism

Minority organizations in our study sample likely suffered disadvantages in obtaining outside support for their projects—loans, some government grants, placement of their trained workers, major customers for their projects, joint venturers, or resident participation.[15] Direct links between race/ethnicity and the loss or limitation of projects are difficult to establish in our study's short site visits. However, signs of less than equal treatment, of lower expectations of success, or other discriminatory responses to minority organizations were provided in a number of interviews with outsiders, referred to by NDO staff, or were otherwise visible.

In part these signs consisted of outsiders' references to minorities with degrading language or negative stereotypes and generalizations—probably largely unconscious references couched in moderated terms, but nonetheless spoken to outside interviewers or to NDO staff, often by people with whom NDOs in fact worked. In part the obvious results of racism were signals such as the stunning lack of public facilities and services in minority neighborhoods compared to nonminority in the same city.

Notably, some predominantly white Anglo NDOs suffered similar treatment, at the hands of people who apparently took the attitude that some collective human impairment must be responsible for their being low income. Some organizations with women as leaders had additional credibility problems. Perhaps the main implied lesson is that NDO work seems still very much to be made more difficult by outsiders' assumptions that their participants, as an identifiable class of people, cannot or will not perform. Our study was not designed to pinpoint project manifestations of this problem; but the signs are clear that racism, sexism, and disdain for disadvantaged people more generally remain real and potent obstacles to NDO development.

---

15. In one instance, some residents were intimidated out of supporting NDO actions by members of the majority.

## 6. Political Conservatism

Political conservatism, in the sense of opposition to assisting NDOs on philosophical grounds, is strong at the local government level in several of the study cases. This attitude presents a barrier to NDOs' attempts to establish working relations with the local government for funding, technical assistance, linkages to other outsiders, and increases in supporting services/ goods for its projects. The attitude was prevalent in only a minority of cases, but in those cases it created major problems, unless sufficient outside funding and assistance could be mustered to counteract it and to begin to break it down through demonstrated success. Sometimes the vocal adoption by NDOs of some constructive elements of "conservative" philosophy, for example, business-like care in developing projects, also contributed to improving relations.

## 7. Timing of Political Events

Many political occurrences beyond the control of individual NDOs substantially affect project funding availability and program options. The coming and going of federal programs clearly has had the broadest impact. The advent of CDBG and CETA programs provided major new sources of funding for expansion by existing NDOs, making specific projects feasible and contributing to core staff support. For some newer organizations, their ability to begin carrying out projects and sometimes their very existence rested fundamentally on these funding sources. Earlier, the "political climate" of civil rights demonstrations and urban riots helped create opportunities for NDOs to garner aid. Conversely, the Nixon housing moratorium was a nearly fatal blow to some older housing-focused NDOs in our sample; and recent CETA cutbacks have reduced the scale of some NDO programs and raised costs in others that used federally paid workers.

In addition, local and national political changes directed toward matters other than program funding affect NDO opportunities. For example, local legislation that tightened enforcement of tax delinquency and housing code rules for landlords provided housing management opportunities for NDOs. And, as mentioned earlier, the federal Community Reinvestment Act seems to have been useful to NDOs in obtaining lender cooperation.

In many cases, these impacts are quite obvious. The points of emphasis are that (1) because the effects of political events can be dramatic, they must be carefully considered in assessing NDO performance, and (2) NDOs may need to seek diverse sources of funding and some financial self-sufficiency to ensure continuing success.

Two more subtle impacts of changes in federal programming also deserve mention. First, replacing one complex program with another strains staff expertise and training for many NDOs which may have concentrated on learning from scratch the operation of a particular program. Second, government administrators themselves have to learn how to tailor actual operations of each new program for successful NDO use.

### 8. Specialized Situations

A host of unique environmental conditions, not included in the above categories, placed obstacles in the paths of sample NDOs or provided them with unusual opportunities. For example, rapid growth in long-distance absentee ownership of neighborhood housing by investors from Southeast Asia, in response to events there, made encouraging private rehabilitation more difficult in one NDO neighborhood. The reluctance of neighborhood residents who plan to return later to their birthplace to become housing owners complicated co-op conversions in another. And the need of a bank to establish a record of community responsibility, after nearly undergoing state receivership for misbehavior, led to use of bank-owned buildings by a third NDO. In evaluating a specific NDO's performance, such factors obviously need to be taken separately into account, though they cannot be categorized.

### 9. A Note on Strategy Response to the Environment

The environmental factors just discussed do not fix in a deterministic way NDOs' abilities to carry out neighborhood revitalization projects. To be sure, such conditions make projects easier or more difficult; and some projects indeed become infeasible because of them. But frequently an NDO's ability to adjust and respond to conditions—to find strategies that build on opportunities and reduce the importance of constraints (or help eliminate them)—is what really proves key.

For example, one study organization faced in succession a housing market of high rents and poor repairs, then landlord abandonment, and then increasing tenant abandonment. This NDO consciously shaped its activities to meet these difficulties. The NDO moved from rent strike organizing to include tenant management and moderate repairs, and then major rehabilitation and new construction, in its undertakings. Other NDOs began land-banking in expectation of displacement pressures, slowly nurtured as yet very modestly fruitful lender elations, or worked to develop housing outside their own overcrowded and high cost neighborhood. This form of responsiveness is an important advantage to the NDOs that practiced it, has led to some difficulties for those that did or could not, and in general greatly influences the actual impact of environmental conditions.

## NON-KEY CHARACTERISTICS

A number of characteristics which we and others expected to be important aspects of an NDO's ability to carry out neighborhood revitalization projects proved either of very limited significance or had very mixed impacts. Of these, written comprehensive long-term planning processes and the personal style of the executive director have previously been noted. Others—the quality of financial recordkeeping, budget/staff size, and turnover in the executive director—are discussed below.

### 1. Quality of Financial Recordkeeping

Quality financial recordkeeping appears to be less of an indicator of NDO project capability than we initially hypothesized. Although NDO staff members suggested that a good financial system was important for attracting and keeping funding, NDOs having a wide range of demonstrated ability in financial recordkeeping were able to successfully carry out neighborhood revitalization projects. In fact, some successful groups operated with inadequate systems (by both their own and some outsider reports) for years.

Financial systems do need to meet some minimum standards. They must be adequate to supply information and documentation specifically required for reports to funding sources. Requirements vary widely, with certain federal programs demanding the most detail. Also, such systems must be sufficient to demonstrate that no funds have been misused. NDO staff frequently cited actual or potential attacks by their enemies focused on funds misappropriation, and they believed that inability to account for monies could be literally fatal for their organizations.

NDO participants also said that financial systems were useful insofar as they provided alerts to budget or cash-flow problems in a timely way and limit the time expended by program staff to supply data. But these elements do not appear central to success, nor do more sophisticated financial planning or management information techniques.

### 2. Budget and Staff Size

We expected budget and staff size to be potentially useful at least as proxies for NDO capability. However, our study showed that, both alone and combined, they provided inadequate information regarding the total energies, skills, and other resources which go into a neighborhood revitalization project. Board, staff, technical assistance providers, and the NDOs as a whole played highly variable roles in project development and implementation. This variability rendered budget and staff size information useful only if measured against the needs of the NDO in its particular situation.

For example, an NDO which has a board of directors involved only in policymaking, minimal volunteer services, and a role to play as its own general contractor has major staff and budget needs. On the other hand, an NDO with a working board, access to major amounts of free technical assistance, and largely a negotiating role in its development project might rely on the local government and developer to provide capital and operating outlays and operate with a small staff and budget. In addition, a large staff and budget say for outreach on a particular project may mean less in terms of overall capability than the presence of one or two key entrepreneurs.

### 3. Change in Executive Director

Our initial hypothesis, supported by the views of several experts, was that turnover in executive directorship would generally be a highly traumatic experience and interfere significantly with NDO organizational and project development. Experience for our sample NDOs was in fact much more mixed.

In several cases, change was smooth and productive. Usually the incoming director had substantial past involvement with the NDO and its leadership. Such involvement created important understanding and trust in advance although these linkages did not guarantee successful transition. And other key staff and board members provided important continuity. In two instances, the new executive directors were NDO founders and board members, one of whom received continuing assistance and advice from his voluntarily departing predecessor. In another, the new executive director was a former city administrator who had worked with the NDO and had skills and contacts needed to rescue the NDO from a crisis situation.

About half of the sample NDOs which underwent changes in executive director had less than smooth transitions and encountered internal conflict. Those NDOs entered periods of lower project activity as they attempted to work out internal relationships and replace the skills and experience of the preceding executive director. Sometimes, an NDO benefited from such an experience in the long run. The experience helped NDO participants reach general agreement on such issues as board/staff powers and NDO strategy (for example, balance of development versus organizing) and increased communication. Even when agreement was reached only after certain factions left an NDO, the impact was a mix of such benefits as increased internal cohesion and losses in areas such as community support or experienced staff. Other times the result was largely a costly delay while the new director developed the range of expertise and trust the predecessor had obtained.

Several of the NDOs studied have undergone no change in executive director during their lifetimes and generally do not have a potential replacement in mind or a formal line of succession. Some but not all of these organizations appear to have developed a safety net in the event of the director's departure—either in close organizational ties with a network of funding and technical assistance sources or in an experienced technically skilled staff member who could lend major assistance to a new executive director. It is difficult to say how well even those NDOs would weather the loss of their strong long-term leadership.

Because this study examined only currently existing, reasonably to greatly successful neighborhood organizations, our findings may be biased. NDOs for whom executive director turnover was extremely traumatic, causing a dramatic interruption of their work, are unlikely to be included. Nonetheless, the evidence at least suggests that staff director transition need not be an overwhelming setback under reasonably favorable circumstances. NDOs' own actions were key to creating those circumstances—actions to deliberately develop potential new leaders and to assure incoming executive directors of support and some elements of continuity.

# III. STAGES OF NDOs' DEVELOPMENT

A scheme for characterizing NDOs' "stages of development"—steps in the growth of their capabilities to carry out revitalization projects—can be valuable for at least three purposes. If we know how to characterize a highly developed neighborhood group, then we can help less advanced NDOs to recognize the capabilities that they should concentrate on building. If we identify some processes through which NDOs typically pass at given points in their history, then both NDOs and their sources of aid can better predict impending problems and expedite organizational growth. And if we also know that NDOs at certain development levels can make good use of particular types of assistance,[1] then identifying stages of development can help in tailoring such aid.

Devising a useful categorization scheme is not easy. We have reduced the complexities somewhat by focusing on NDOs' abilities to carry out revitalization projects, rather than on all aspects of their organizational growth; but many difficulties remain. One possible way to categorize NDOs is to define them as more and less advanced according to their past success as measured in a single, tangible way. For example, the number and scope of revitalization projects successfully completed (output targets met, costs reasonable) in a recent period might be used to categorize these organizations. The problem, aside from difficulties of measuring success even in simple terms, is that this approach is not very useful for the purposes just outlined. Simply knowing which NDOs have a substantial history of successful projects does not tell us how to develop the capacity for success in other organizations.

Another way of categorizing stages of development is to identify a common train of events and changing characteristics which, *in consistent time sequence,* describes the process of development of many different NDOs. For example, we could seek to characterize a first stage of development by a long list of events that NDOs generally experience and capacities they generally build in the early periods of organizational life. We could make similar lists for later time periods.

The problem with this approach, our study evidence strongly suggests, is that the notion of consistent time sequencing is contrary to fact. Even among the 12 NDOs we studied, the timing of major elements of growth is diverse. Some NDOs were project-oriented development groups from their start, acquired technically competent staff at an early point, and later struggled to deepen roots in the community. Others began as advocacy groups with strong constituent bases, concentrated on providing services and hiring

---

1. Chapter 4 of this paper suggests some connections between level of NDO development and appropriate technical and financial assistance.

neighborhood people in their early programming efforts, and built technical competence for physical and economic development projects after years of other work. Some developed single, major project lines until their efforts were large, highly competent, and widely recognized. Others diversified very early. Some struggled through internal disputes over objectives and roles soon after community development projects became a part of their agenda. For others, such struggles came either before or long after development work began; and for still others it has not occurred at all, at least to date. In sum, many combinations of capabilities, in terms of the key characteristics such as those described in chapter 2, appeared even in our small sample. Subdividing the NDOs according to their early beginnings—in advocacy, service delivery, development, or a mixture—sorts out some but by no means all of these differences in characteristics over time. Neat sequencing simply is not an appropriate description.

A further approach to categorizing stages of development is to identify important common processes that many NDOs do pass through at *some* time in their lives and that seem to lead to more successful and sophisticated revitalization project development. This identification can be made without trying to describe any single, complete time line of development. The common processes we have in mind here are not themselves individual key elements of capacity such as strong leadership, political clout, and the other elements, described in chapter 2. Instead, they are dynamic occurrences involving multiple changes in NDO outlook, knowledge, experience, and a range of specific capabilities. NDOs may work through the processes, or parts of them, in quite different time sequences. Still, if we identify key processes correctly, we can categorize NDOs that have worked through more of the processes, more completely, as being at more advanced levels of development. The notion of common processes differing in timing is consistent with our observations, and identifying such processes based on study site visits and related research appears feasible. Using this concept of stages of development also contributes to meeting the objectives of categorizing NDOs' development levels as previously outlined.

Finally, a fourth approach to stages of development is to look at NDO growth in terms of the development of individual key characteristics of capacity already discussed in chapter 2, particularly internal capabilities and relations to outsiders. We can do this without suggesting that the timing of their development is similar across NDOs or that sets of characteristics tend to develop neatly together. We can trace the growth of each characteristic separately and describe its process and levels of development. We can then categorize NDOs with many well-developed individual characteristics as relatively more advanced. Insofar as the characteristics considered really are key to successful project work, the approach is valuable in helping to structure outside aid and internal development processes.

This chapter describes NDO stages of development by combining the last two approaches. We first describe a set of processes that appear to be common elements of NDO growth, though in differing time sequences. We then discuss the development process for specific key capacities that characterize organizations as they mature. From this study's point of view, we consider NDOs that have worked through many of the processes and have many well-developed key capacities to be more advanced organizations. NDOs, and their sources of assistance, should be able to use the processes and levels of development of particular capacities identified here, together with the full list of key characteristics discussed in chapter 2, to assess NDOs' current states of advancement. Such an assessment should help determine the kinds of further capacity development the neighborhood organizations most need. This assessment can also help determine the scope of project activities which NDOs can successfully pursue and for which they can effectively use assistance.

## COMMON PROCESSES

The following pages identify and describe seven processes that seem common to NDO growth patterns, according to the evidence from our study. The processes may be observed at different organizational ages, but they nonetheless represent steps in development of NDOs' capabilities.

Some of the processes identified generally occur relatively early in NDO life. Our evidence that they are common to most NDOs is the strongest. They are shared by a substantial majority of study NDOs—currently for young NDOs and as part of organizational history for others. Other processes identified as usually occurring later are shared by most of our organizations with longer and stronger project histories. They are either underway or under discussion in some of the less experienced groups. And in general they have not yet occurred in the remaining less mature NDOs. The evidence that these later processes are common among NDOs is, however, weaker. We cannot be certain that younger NDOs will in fact repeat them in similar fashion as they grow, even though they may seem poised to do so.

The list of processes is not exhaustive. A larger set of study NDOs may have produced a larger number of clear patterns. And, again, many growth patterns are best described as the development of individual key characteristics of capacity, discussed separately in chapter 2 and in "Development of Key Characteristics of Capacity" in this chapter. The seven key processes we have identified are the following:

- Formally establishing an organization
- Deciding to carry out programs and to create institutions
- Confronting the difficulties of early neighborhood revitalization projects

- Becoming competent in specific project work
- Developing a network of relations with outsiders
- Building a diverse range of projects
- Institutionalizing expanded project competence

We discuss each of these in turn below.

## 1. Formally Establishing an Organization

Many of our sample NDOs existed as informal groups of political, and sometimes programmatic activists significantly prior to forming independent organizations. Groups of individuals met to discuss and plan approaches to pressing community issues, lobbied, protested, and/or worked in electoral campaigns. The groups carried out these activities before taking on any identifiable name or structure and before incorporating, establishing by-laws, or following other procedures that characterize formal organizations. Precursors of a few of the NDOs actually carried out revitalization projects of the types we are focusing on in this study—for example, tenement housing repairs—before setting up organizations.

But, as discussed in chapter 2, formally establishing nonprofit corporations was important to NDOs for several purposes, including qualifying for funding and attracting membership and board directors. And establishing a clear identity, creating ways to set policy (particularly forming boards of directors), and designating some staff (paid or unpaid) to carry out chosen activities proved necessary early elements for future project work. It is important to remember, however, that many NDOs went through this process of formal establishment as part of building their advocacy or social service capabilities, sometimes long before they undertook neighborhood revitalization projects as more narrowly defined for this study.

## 2. Deciding to Carry Out Programs and Create Institutions

Many NDOs, examined in this study and cited elsewhere by other experts, did not initially assume that they themselves would undertake programs and projects. In numerous cases, the NDOs came to carry out those activities as a result of a learning process. Their experiences in advocacy—urging governmental bodies to address community problems more adequately—proved unsatisfactory. They found some legislators and administrators unwilling to provide the necessary effort and resources. Agencies were sometimes unable to deliver successfully the efforts that were authorized. These agencies lacked the understanding of special community needs, the contacts with wary residents, and the commitment to deal with difficult conditions that NDOs can often contribute. The will and/or skill to revise programs to fit special neighborhood conditions were often missing in government while at least potentially present in the community. Out of dissatisfaction with repeated shortfalls in service and project delivery, until success could no longer be expected, arose the NDOs' movement toward carrying out projects through their own direct efforts.

Sometimes this process of deciding to take on projects took place very early in organizational life. Perhaps the decision resulted from dissatisfaction with government action on one or two high priority issues. The early decision was especially likely for organizations with a community development project-type set of interests from the outset. Other times the decision grew more slowly from a changing understanding of what community needs were in contrast to what government might provide. At times a decision involved substantial internal disagreement about whether and how big a role programming, and especially community development projects, should play in an organization's agenda. In any case it was a clearly common, experience-based passage for organizations of the kinds involved in our study. Once the process was substantially completed, NDOs could begin to focus on the additional hard work needed actually to deliver programs themselves.

### 3. Confronting the Difficulties of Early Neighborhood Revitalization Projects

NDOs taking on their first neighborhood revitalization projects frequently found the work a good deal more difficult than they had anticipated. Learning from early project experiences to establish realistic expectations, identify and start to build needed capabilities, and anticipate some likely problems is a common first step in developing effective program delivery.[2] NDOs' increasing understanding of the capabilities and actions needed to carry out projects successfully forms the basis for later steps to pursue them.

Early project experience taught our study NDOs to lower their expectations of how quickly projects could be completed and to raise their expectations of cost. They learned how to estimate and then to seek resources more adequate to the proposed work and how to avoid promising more than they could deliver to their members and community constituents.

NDOs also gained some improved sense of the kinds of technical expertise that are required to design and implement projects. Many recognized, after one or a few projects, that some needed special skills were not available from their current staff and would have to be obtained by well-targeted training or recruitment. Through their early projects, NDOs began to discover the usefulness of getting aid and information from outsiders when "learn by doing" was too slow and costly. And at the same time they saw

---

2. Some other specific ways that early project experience contributes to capacity building, particularly training staff and transferring skills from technical assistance sources, are discussed further under "Development of Key Characteristics of Capacity" in this chapter and in chapter 4. The focus here is not on building key characteristics but on recognizing needs.

the difficulties of controlling that assistance without careful advance planning and continuous care.

In addition, early projects taught NDOs' staff that they needed to make extensive efforts in order to keep board members and community residents educated about the neighborhood development process and satisfied with its progress. The major obstacles that neighborhood environments placed in the paths of their projects caused many NDOs to begin to choose work more adaptive to external conditions. For example, instead of trying to generate jobs solely through the difficult routes of attracting or creating independent new enterprises, some NDOs developed employment in the process of meeting basic resident needs (e.g., in housing maintenance and management). And the whole range of difficulties NDOs encountered taught them to try to predict and plan for possible problems and leave some flexibility for continued surprises.

These lessons combined gave NDOs the knowledge and perspective to work effectively at filling their critical capacity-building needs as they moved on to further projects.

### 4. Becoming Competent in Specific Project Work

A logical next step in NDO growth is to become systematically and consistently effective at carrying out one or a few types of revitalization projects. Recognizing the difficulties and needs inherent in these projects provides impetus and direction for NDOs to build toward effective project work. Actually becoming effective in neighborhood revitalization, however, requires developing a host of key capacities, through experience and deliberate capacity-creation efforts. We have described the key capacities in chapter 2, and we discuss their individual growth processes under "Development of Key Characteristics of Capacity." There is no reason to attempt a summary of that analysis here. The point is simply that, for NDOs examined in this study, a key element in the growth process is to follow up recognition of the difficulties of project activity with positive action. NDOs must carefully develop needed capabilities and then convert that capacity into implementation of projects. Some NDOs are slower to come to this competency, perhaps because of other priorities or lack of resources; but their continued growth as neighborhood development-type organizations is dependent on ultimately gaining it.

### 5. Developing a Network of Relations with Outsiders

Successful NDOs continuously develop a network of people and institutions they can draw on for various forms of assistance and support, throughout the other steps in their growth. The networks include sources of funding and technical assistance, political allies and advisors, potential project co-participants largely from the private sector, and other NDOs or similar public interest groups. Early in their existence, NDOs are dependent on a few of these connections and the linkages they provide to additional outsiders. Gradually, NDOs learn how and where to find a greater variety of other forms of assistance on their own and nurture their expanding contacts. At an advanced level, NDOs can draw on their networks for established sources of aid in relation to a wide variety of needs. And funding sources, allies, and coventurers begin to come to capable NDOs with proposals as well.

For successful NDOs we observed directly or indirectly, much of the development of relations is deliberate—for example, designed to build capacity in fundraising or in political clout. Indeed, recognizing the importance of establishing a network of contacts and learning how to build it are parts of NDO maturation.

The process of creating a multipurpose network is essentially a combination of building relations with various outsiders as described piece by piece in chapter 2 and later in this chapter. The individual importance of the various linkages is detailed. What is emphasized here is the value of putting an extensive network into place, so that an NDO can think systematically about its needs for aid in particular situations and call upon appropriate and tested agents of assistance.

### 6. Building a Diverse Range of Projects

NDOs in this study generally grew in their ability to control the selection of projects and to widen the variety of projects which they considered and undertook. Many began their project work in a particular area of long-identified community need, by reacting to and taking advantage of a funding opportunity. Several found that they lacked important internal capabilities or external links, restricting their development of one initial or intended line of work and forcing them into another. In general, external and internal conditions controlled project selection at early stages.

But gradually, for the more advanced organizations, several changes took place. NDOs came to recognize the importance of picking projects that made special contributions to their strategies for neighborhood revitalization,[3] rather than simply reacting to opportunities. At least from time to time, the organizations were able to use their track records, personal contacts, and other capabilities to bring in the resources required to meet the needs that these NDOs had specifically identified. Maturing NDOs also usually diversified their projects though some did this much later in their revitalization project histories than did others. NDOs became more conscious of the interplay of needs in their communities. Some, for example, tried to develop employment projects to give people the resources necessary to afford the housing improvements that NDO projects were making. Advanced NDOs were able to build or attract sufficient capacity to handle the new

---

3. For example, they selected key anchor buildings for NDO rehabilitation as a means of generating wider private reinvestment.

lines of work and again to use past track record and outside relationships to attract needed aid.

In increasing their powers of both selection and diversification, NDOs began taking direct advantage of the expanded set of their own projects. Their operations became large enough to train and employ significant numbers of local workers within the organizations themselves, so that all kinds of NDO work became forms of economic development. NDOs traded explicitly on their success in one area of work to gain participation in another. For example, an NDO was able to bring a housing rehabilitation project into its neighborhood and share in its profits, in significant part because the organization offered a strong record of success in managing housing and thus an ability to sustain the project once renovation was complete. And NDOs began to carry out new functions that had been performed for their earlier projects by outsiders, for example, brokering their own real estate transactions or managing their own housing rehabilitation and construction projects. Bringing those functions in-house both increased the productivity of outside funds[4] and provided one principal means for developing profit- or surplus-producing activities.

### 7. *Institutionalizing Expanded Project Competence*

In "tooling up" for expanded project activities like those just described, and in carrying them out, NDOs tried to institutionalize the internal capacities needed for continuing success. This meant, among other things, creating organizational structures that fit expanded operations and establishing means to maintain skill levels once they were obtained. For example, executive directors (often slowly) delegated increased responsibilities, staff members were assigned special areas of work, second level and back-up managers were developed, and boards of directors were reorganized into working committees along functional lines. Efforts were made to retain valuable staff, for example, by improving salaries.

The process of institutionalization is one of developing means to handle expanded project loads over the long term, without losing the ingredients of quality work that were present when much of an NDO's entire store of energy was poured into one or two projects. For most organizations in our sample, this process is still very much an early or continuing one.

## Differing Sequences

Having discussed a set of dynamic processes, we reemphasize that even these seven broadly defined steps occur in differing sequence for various NDOs. We believe that the number of processes that are well advanced helps to measure an NDO's stage of development and that some processes usually precede others. But we do not expect organizations to move through

---

4. See "The Role of Funding," in chapter 4 for further discussion.

them systematically in the order of our presentation. Our sample of study NDOs provides clear evidence of the diversity in sequences of growth.

For example, two of our organizations of similarly substantial success and longevity nonetheless followed very disparate maturation routes. Their growth patterns are summarized in the two parts of figure 1. In the first case, residents set up as an organization and decided to undertake programs almost simultaneously (process #1 and #2), in response to a project opportunity arising externally but highly consistent with their community needs. Almost immediately the NDO faced the day-to-day problems of taking on community development work with minimal experience (#3). Over the next several years, the NDO gradually built a strong capability in the area in which its work began, with increasingly experienced staff, involvement in a variety of closely related programs, and expanding credibility with city government and the community. This maturation is illustrated as becoming competent in a chosen line of work and developing a network of outside relations (#4 and #5). Later, as the scale of activity grew, the NDO began to institutionalize its expanded competence (#6). For example, the NDO trained and developed middle level managers and took over program functions that they had previously contracted out. Now one of the largest enterprises/institutions in its community, the NDO has only more recently diversified widely from its main line of project activity (#7).

In the second example, an NDO's future participants established a network of relations (#5) through their advocacy and organizing efforts— linking community residents, political allies, and funding sources—well before the NDO itself came to exist. The NDO later became a formal organization but worked more slowly than in our first example toward delivering programs itself (#1 and #2). Starting in social service, the NDO did not for several more years really add community development work as an additional focus (#3). But this organization rather quickly diversified its development efforts, once begun (#7). The NDO is now working hard to overcome the problems of getting several types of projects rolling simultaneously. Developing strong competency in a line(s) of work (#4) and institutionalizing such competence (#6) are still somewhat down the road.

Both of the example NDOs have clearly moved, through processes we have discussed, to more advanced stages of development since their birth. We can identify and measure (qualitatively) that progress though it takes distinct forms in these and other NDOs.

## DEVELOPMENT OF KEY CHARACTERISTICS OF CAPACITY

To a significant extent, the discussion of key internal characteristics and relations to outsiders in chapter 2 already provides another means to catego-

# FIGURE 1

## GROWTH PATTERNS OF TWO NEIGHBORHOOD DEVELOPMENT ORGANIZATIONS (NDOs)

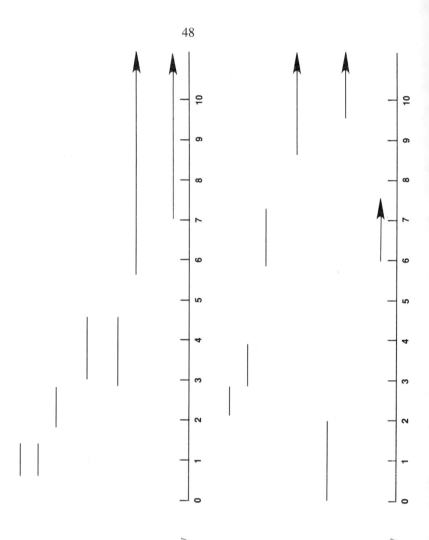

*First NDO*

1. Formally establishing an organization
2. Deciding to carry out programs
3. Confronting the difficulties of early community development projects
4. Becoming competent in a specific area of community development work
5. Developing a network of relations
6. Institutionalizing expanded competence in community development
7. Building a range of projects

Years of Activity

*Second NDO*

1. Formally establishing an organization
2. Deciding to carry out programs
3. Confronting the difficulties of early community development projects
4. Becoming competent in a specific area of community development work
5. Developing a network of relations
6. Institutionalizing expanded competence in community development
7. Building a range of projects

Years of Activity

rize NDOs' levels of advancement. NDOs with "long" track records, "strong" in-house technical competence, and "deep" roots in the community are more advanced than those which lack them. The larger the number of key characteristics that are well developed, and the stronger each capability is, the more advanced the organization is. Chapter 2 identifies characteristics that matter, indicates the influences they may have, and pinpoints some of the elements of each characteristic that signify its being well developed—giving meaning to "long," "strong," or "deep."

We would gain little by reiterating the full list of characteristics and reciting, for example, that a medium level of political clout represents a middle level of development of that characteristic. And, as already indicated above, our research does not support the notion of picking a single combination[5] of development levels of characteristics to serve as the definition of early or middle or advanced capacity development. A given capacity level may result from various combinations of the many key characteristics that were developed in different sequences by different NDOs.

Instead, we discuss the growth process of *individual* key characteristics, in order to make more concrete the progression of levels to which each may be developed in various NDOs and to contribute to an understanding of how the growth in each element of capacity might be encouraged. We discuss only a subset of the internal and outside-relations characteristics of chapter 2.[6] Our focus is on those for which our research has identified some significant, specific levels of development.[7] Other characteristics either do not reveal a well-defined continuum of development identifiable within the case studies of this research or are more "inherited" than developed. Such characteristics receive brief attention below or are disregarded.

## 1. Internal Characteristics

### a. Paid, full-time staff with development expertise

As described in chapter 2, creating in-house capability in project development and implementation is a critical element of capacity growth. Pieces of this process are reasonably identifiable for our sample of NDOs. Again, all groups need not pass through all stages or move at the same pace.

At earliest stages, an NDO's level of technical expertise generally depends on the skills and experience the executive director (very likely the

---

5. The research does not even support choosing a narrow set of combinations.

6. And we disregard the environmental conditions, because they are clearly not elements of NDO capacity-development.

7. Given NDOs will not necessarily have moved through all of the levels but may have skipped from one point to another and moved at different points in organizational life. But each appears to represent an identifiable level of capacity.

only non-support-staff person) has.[8] How extensive these skills and experiences were varied widely among our sample NDOs. In any case, even the most skilled director at some point became unable to handle both project detail and all of his/her other tasks. An additional staff member was then hired, usually from the local community, to perform project development and implementation tasks, often for a specific project or group of similar projects on which an NDO was proceeding. In most instances, this person had some orientation toward community development/neighborhood revitalization work but limited if any direct training and experience in carrying out development projects.[9] Several NDOs hired people with education in urban planning. These staffers provided help in understanding some parts of the development process but usually still needed to learn many aspects of entrepreneurship, packaging, and implementation. At this level, an NDO may be seen as having expanded energy for technical work and increased potential for staff capacity development but still very limited actual technical capacity.

An NDO's development staffer typically becomes more knowledgeable gradually. The staffer actually plans and carries out a project and shares the learning process with the executive director and other staff or board members, asks questions of outsiders, learns by doing (and erring), and sometimes receives technical assistance that not only performs tasks but demonstrates how they can later be done in-house.[10] If the staff member is a reasonably good learner, this process creates a distinctly higher level of capability for future work. As indicated in chapter 2, the major steps and details in moving a project forward are much better handled by a person with specific previous experience in identifying and performing the required tasks.

Several NDOs that we studied had failures in technical staff development at early stages. Some people were unable to learn skills and develop projects at an adequate pace and were forced out. NDOs were left with delayed projects and repeated needs for recruitment or training-from-scratch. Some staff members learned but left for other work.

Where such failures did not occur, an NDO developed a staff person (or occasionally persons) at work long enough to become quite competent in technical project work, thought not yet able to do more sophisticated work in packaging or implementing new projects. Trained staff might or might not, however, have the perhaps more innate potential to fill the

---

8. This may be supplemented by the expertise of active board members or perhaps technical assistance available from the outset, but we want to concentrate here on internal staff capacity.

9. More particularly, it is unlikely the staff person has experience with the specific kind of project the NDO was currently undertaking.

10. Project-oriented technical assistance is discussed in detail in chapter 4.

organization's entrepreneurial and technical growth needs. These needs include the abilities to identify new project opportunities consistent with NDO goals and environment and to develop a wider array of technical skills. Some of the staff people did become fully equipped technical experts (described more fully in chapter 2). Such growth in competence depended not only on specific experience and individual capacity but also on the NDO's deliberate creation of training opportunities (e.g., carefully involving a key staff member in each step of a joint venturer's work).

Alternatively, an NDO might recognize the need to recruit a talented and experienced outsider[11] to fill the role of fully equipped technical staff. The advice of technical assistance providers who had close links to an NDO was sometimes helpful in determining whether and when outside hiring was necessary. The decision to recruit from outside needed to be coupled with realistic recruitment practices (salaries, qualifications, area of search).

Such a decision was often controversial, involving extended discussions and some disagreements among staff, board, and other community members. But outside recruitment could be a successful means to obtain expertise. Important conditions for success are that the new staff person be taught to understand community needs and not be allowed to use technical knowledge to dominate policymaking,[12] and that people from the community be given other staff opportunities on the staff. Neither the training nor recruitment approach proved systematically preferable. Each was capable of producing the next level of broader technical skill and experience.

The final recognizable element of developing staff technical expertise is the expansion of these skills within the NDO. One part of that is broadening competence into more than one development area. In particular for the NDOs we studied, staff expertise in physical development was not immediately convertible to economic development projects. Skills in economic development instead had to be pursued separately through similar processes. Either a single staffer needed to gain wider experience, or additional experts had to be trained or recruited in new areas of work.

A second part of expansion is institutional deepening of expertise. Middle level managers had to be trained, in order for an NDO to carry out an expanded set of projects now and in the future. Training middle level staff from within the community was particularly important to maintain community support for NDOs recruiting a top technical person from outside. A third part of expansion, for very large organizations, is to increase the *num-*

---

11. Outside the NDO and perhaps, but not necessarily, also outside the NDO's community.

12. Strong executive directors conscious of these needs, and strong community-based boards, were the best assurances of these conditions for successful outside recruitment. But some outside recruits failed. They could not be trained to fit in with the community or they lacked the expected skills.

*ber* of trained people in primary and middle level technical roles. Both the deepening of expertise at the middle management level and the expansion of numbers at top levels are especially important to ensure against damage to capacity if a particular key staffer leaves. Several NDOs gained relatively little from the processes of individuals' skill development just described because of turnover of key staff who had not adequately shared learning.

### b. Track record

Obviously, NDOs' track records grow over time as the organizations successfully complete additional projects. There does not appear to be a series of neat quantitative cut-off points at which the impact of a track record on external impressions and internal learning changes markedly.

An exception is successful completion of the first community development/neighborhood revitalization project. That first effort seems to do much to increase an NDO's visibility in and trust from the community, the skills of staff in at least one line of work, understanding of the development process, and credibility with outside sources of funds.[13] The first development project apparently marks a useful separation between the NDOs in very early stages of movement into community development and those more advanced.

Nonetheless, important differences exist between NDOs whose first revitalization project is also its first major activity as an organization and those that have a significant history of advocacy actions or social service programming. All NDOs learn much about the nitty-gritty of development projects in their first project of that type. But those with a history of other activities may have already built credibility and support with community and outsiders, gained understanding of the need for skilled staff, and developed a sense of the detailed planning and implementation work necessary for any substantial project.

It proved difficult to identify just what kind of track record, in terms of project types and NDOs' role in them,[14] is important to reap the benefits of successful past performance discussed in chapter 2. We were able to draw some tentative conclusions about the relation of track record to attracting outside support and to training staff. Our best inferences suggest that potential private lenders and coventurers look relatively narrowly at experience. They wanted to see past success in the particular types of projects and roles that NDOs were proposing to undertake with help from them. In terms of ability to attract participation from the private sector, therefore, NDOs with diversified track records are more fully developed. Government support, on the other hand, seemed more easily attracted by past program experience of

---

13. The last three of these occur only if projects are not dominated by outside contractors oblivious to the process of in-house capacity building.

14. Planner, coordinator, monitor, packager, developer, manager.

kinds other than those newly proposed. Government was willing to give substantial credit for successful performance in another area of work. In addition, both private and public sectors prefer to support projects not much larger than those with which an NDO was experienced. Those actors and NDO staff saw taking on larger-scale projects as a next step in the development of relatively advanced organizations.

The carryover of staff learning across project types can be substantial in terms of increased understanding of the process of development. But to gain specific technical knowledge and skills, learning experiences must include participation in quite closely related projects and roles or be supplemented with substantial technical assistance. Because technical staff knowledge is partly project-specific, an NDO's development level is connected to diversity of staff experience. Carryover of skill development seemed greater between types of development projects than from social services to development, but it proved difficult to find really conclusive evidence of this greater transfer.

*c. Leadership by an effective executive director*

Many of the most important characteristics of strong leadership by executive directors do not appear to be developed during NDO growth but seem to exist, latent or active, within individuals who form or join these organizations. Abilities to identify opportunities, pursue them resourcefully, shape and share organizational vision with others, and deal effectively with outsiders may have sharpened and matured with NDO experience. But they were also clearly strengths of impressive leaders of very young NDOs and of incoming new directors in older organizations.

Leadership elements that do seem to grow with NDO experience include the executive director's own confidence. Increased confidence allowed directors to delegate more authority, better share decision making with board members, and make more convincing presentations to outsiders. In addition, the credibility of and trust in the executive director grew with experience for both insiders and outsiders. A sense of the importance of adequate NDO management and attention to capacity building seemed also to arise partly out of experience. But in the main, NDOs seem best described as "advanced" in terms of executive director leadership whenever they have a highly qualified[15] person in charge. This development may occur at various points in organizational life and has little to do with other conditions.

*d. Record of doing homework*

Successful NDOs generally develop increased concern for and skill in careful performance of "homework" tasks as part of a learning process. As

---

15. See "Leadership by an Effective Executive Director" chapter 2 for further description of important talents of the executive director.

discussed further in chapter 4, many organizations at early stages of their work imported homework skills in writing and in preparing material to meet funding requirements ( as well as more specific technical skills). These skills were gradually developed in-house through both the experience of working with the technical assistance providers and through outside hiring. Bringing proposal writing and related skills in-house puts NDOs in the distinctly more advanced position of being able to control their own fund-seeking processes. NDOs learned from their own experience, by asking questions, and occasionally from painful error, the steps in bureaucratic processes for obtaining project support or approval. This learning usually took place fairly early in an NDO's history. Even NDOs only moderately advanced by other standards had a good understanding of the presentations, deadlines, and decision points involved in seeking CDBG funds, for example. And these NDOs could grasp a new funding process with relative ease.

Predicting budget needs accurately was more difficult to learn. NDOs frequently underestimated costs and timing in carrying out projects, because they lacked specific similar project experience and adequate records of costs for what past work existed. A *first* community development-type project was often extremely valuable in increasing an NDO's understanding of realistic costs and especially of timing, regardless of the specific kind of work. Thereafter, however, more advanced learning seemed to require significant experience with projects similar to those that were being currently undertaken.

For each of the processes of learning to carry out homework tasks, the executive director's commitment to having good homework often seemed important in speeding development. Directors impressed staff members with the importance of detail and gave key staff people responsibility for seeing that homework tasks were completed.

NDOs found substantial advantage in establishing a continuing *history* of doing good homework and making that history known to outsiders. Successfully establishing such a history represents a further level of advancement of "homework" capacity. We encountered several instances in which government administrators were eager to inform specific NDOs about funding opportunities and aid them in applying. A principal reason was that the organizations were expected, on the basis of past performance, to write proposals that fulfilled requirements, to develop needed political support systematically, to meet reporting requirements, and to carry out other homework tasks. NDOs drew assistance because they could be counted on to help meet agencies' objectives of efficiently putting available project money to work.

### e. Board/staff relations

The development of board-staff relations was described in detail in chapter 2, especially in terms of gaining agreement on roles and objectives. To review, maturing board/staff relations include establishing processes for hiring and firing staff, assigning detailed programmatic tasks to staff and policymaking and support-creating roles to the board, and creating program priorities for the NDO that are shared by board and staff. We further examine how this development occurs both in chapter 2 and in the technical assistance portion of this chapter.

What we want to emphasize here is that the timing of progress in board/ staff relations varies widely among NDOs. A few NDOs seem to achieve a consensus on priorities and division of responsibility when they first form. These NDOs' main task in promoting board/staff relation is to communicate and maintain that common view as board or staff turnover occurs or new program opportunities are identified. Preexisting personal relationships between the executive director and board chairperson contributed heavily to such early agreements.

In many other instances, effort at working out board/staff relationships was triggered by events such as expanding NDO staff from a very small base (reducing the need for certain day-to-day work by board members) or changing executive directors (defining the powers of the new recruit). Perhaps the most common trigger was a disagreement over the merits of and authority for firing a community staff member or hiring an outsider. Issues of program focus also served as triggers, when community development activities came to compete with work on advocacy and social services, when NDOs sought outside aid from new sources, or when organizations contemplated profit-seeking efforts. How good relationships are between board and staff at a point in an NDO's history depends heavily on whether and when triggering of events of these types occur and lead to the establishment of cooperative arrangements.

### f. Financial recordkeeping

While our study has not identified this characteristic as being particularly key to NDO project success, financial record-keeping capability does show a fairly systematic growth process among our sample NDOs. This process is described in detail in chapter 4 in discussing the role of technical assistance in supporting it.

## 2. Relations with the Community and Relevant Outside Actors

### a. Roots in the community

Our research offers no definitive insights on means for defining strength ("level of advancement") of an NDO's roots in the community. Even other researchers' and practitioners' efforts directed to that topic alone have not revealed clear definitions. Our work has tried to make specific some of the ways roots are important to NDO development (see chapter 2). That process does suggest some possible indicators of levels of community links. These might include ability to get people to participate directly in NDO policymaking, program efforts (as workers or recipients), or related advocacy actions; understanding by an NDO of its community's current project priorities and programming needs; development of a process for continued community input and redefinition of priorities; and a willingness of community members to "go to bat" for the NDO when needed. Obviously, there are no neat cutoff points between early, intermediate, and advanced stages in building these connections.

What is clear is that community roots develop at differing stages in organizational life, through various means. Some NDOs brought deep roots to their creation: they were coalitions of existing organizations or groups of trusted community activists or local merchants. For further development, these NDOs needed mechanisms to keep coalition members involved with the organizations' projects. Other organizations evolved as advocacy groups and actively involved large numbers of community residents in visible joint efforts. Additional effort was needed to explain to residents the reasons for undertaking their own neighborhood revitalization projects and to help give them enough understanding and control of the community development process to maintain their participation.

An effective mechanism for preserving and strengthening community roots for NDOs with coalition or advocacy backgrounds was to assure that the NDOs' boards of directors were directly representative of the community, given real decision-making powers, and encouraged to keep their own constituencies informed. Building-by-building tenant representation on the boards of NDOs providing housing management, rehabilitation, and construction is a successful example of means to retain community links. Like other approaches, it requires continuing training of board members.

Other NDOs form and initiate efforts at project development without having strong preexisting community roots. Their growth processes necessarily involved painstaking development of support by including community people in project planning and implementation and by creating visible successes. Roots developed much later relative to internal technical strengths than for other models. These NDOs especially, but other groups as well, seemed to benefit by running some programs which directly benefit large numbers of individuals (e.g., housing counseling, housing management, social services) in addition to whatever slower, less widespread physical and economic development efforts were underway.

### b. Personal relations with funding sources

As indicated in chapter 2, NDO staff and board members often bring valuable preexisting funding source contacts to an organization, at the time of its formation or at some other early point when they first join in its work.

Carefully following up on the funding potential these contacts afford, by moving from chats to meetings to proposals without losing the personal aspects of interaction, represents a first level of sophistication in these relations. A next step is to identify systematically a set of individuals in key funding positions and methodically establish personal contacts with them. Identifying such contacts can be a significant task. It requires choosing appropriate institutions and then working through their staffs or boards to find the decisionmakers. [16] NDOs in active pursuit of such a second round of contacts, in line with well-defined plans, are at a recognizably more advanced level of development of these links. Among our sample NDOs, tactics included paying repeated informational and get-acquainted visits to outsiders well before making funding proposals; joining committees where contacts might be begun; and in some cases (mainly for private sector sources) inviting key individuals to join an NDO's board of directors.

NDOs that pursued deliberate strategies for developing personal contacts generally gained valuable results. Key funders assessed their executive directors' talents very positively. These funders introduced the NDO directors to other funding sources and also notified the directors of special opportunities. At the same time, the NDOs obtained a better understanding of the factors that cause individual funders to provide support and used that information in presenting successful proposals.

### c. Political clout

NDOs' level of political clout must be measured, like the clout of other groups, by obvious yet subtle-to-quantify strengths such as ability to influence legislative and administrative decisions and to place allies in positions of power. Our study did not seek to establish standard categories for those measurements.

We did identify some of the steps through which NDO actors often move to gain clout, as described below. We also found that young NDOs differ significantly in the political knowledge and experience with which they begin their work. And we discovered that NDOs vary in whether certain steps in the process of building clout occurred solely from internal impetus or were speeded by involving experienced outsiders.

A few of our sample NDOs had to begin by learning that political influence matters in neighborhood revitalization work. At the outset, they counted on the soundness of their proposed activities to gain them support. They later discovered that political clout also played a key role in obtaining aid and had to adjust their efforts accordingly. A more common need was

---

16. See chapter 4 for discussion of how technical assistance groups can be of aid in shortening this process.

for NDOs to learn the political process by which decisions were made[17] and then to identify the pressure points accessible to them.

The process of actually gaining influence, of course, included a mix of advocacy (e.g., shows of numbers turned out) and participation by visible NDO individuals in electoral processes (partly politics, election committees, key local commissions, registering and getting out the vote in their own community). Some NDOs fostered candidates from their own ranks in early years of their existence and others did not. We found no pattern to distinguish NDOs that chose to promote their own candidates.

An important element of gaining clout was often largely implicit. NDOs that grew to serve and employ large numbers of people in their programs and whose projects were visible in the community were presumed to have significant potential electoral power through contact and patronage. Political actors sought their favor as a result. Interest in the political potency of employment and service delivery created difficulties as well as opportunities. In some instances, politicians attempted to promote their own political ends by pressuring NDOs to share selection of employees or program recipients with them.

A track record of successful programs and projects also helped develop clout with elected and appointed officials, who hoped to share credit for future successes. Offering credit-sharing was one way NDOs that recognized this potential opportunity developed working relations with politicians who differed from them in basic political outlook.

### d. Relations with private lenders

The reluctance of private institutions to make non-risk-free loans for NDO-sponsored projects was discussed as a common condition of NDOs' environments in chapter 2. While NDOs had relatively little success obtaining loan funds, several were pursuing strategies to garner them, by combining several capabilities discussed elsewhere in the paper. NDOs established personal contacts with high-ranking lending institution officials. These NDOs took advantage of chance encounters and any deliberate opportunities that third parties (e.g., the Federal Home Loan Bank Board) might create. In entering into normal business relations with lenders (e.g., establishing checking and savings accounts, purchasing payroll services) they took pains to perform with businesslike efficiency. NDOs sought and accepted the kinds of assistance, other than loans involving private risk, that lenders were more willing to provide. In those dealings, they were careful to portray qualities lenders were perceived to appreciate: for example, referring only well-

---

17. This step in clout building overlaps with our previous discussion of elements of "homework."

qualified applicants for bank job openings, or repaying short-term operating loans on time. And NDOs sought small project loans, sometimes risk-free as a result of public sector guarantees, through which they could demonstrate to lenders their internal competence and the economic viability of their proposed efforts. Often at the same time, NDOs left partly unconcealed the threat of direct protest against lenders who failed to invest in their neighborhoods. NDOs also took advantage of new regulatory processes if lenders would not cooperate. In many cases, however, it still remains to be seen whether the combination of these tactics will produce substantial loans of lenders' own at-risk funds.

### e. Effective use of technical assistance

The ability to use technical assistance effectively differs among NDOs and often grows with experience. The types of technical assistance that are valuable to NDOs vary substantially with the level of internal NDO development. These subjects are examined in detail in chapter 4.

# IV. FUNDING SUPPORT AND TECHNICAL ASSISTANCE

Funding and technical assistance for NDOs are extremely limited. For that reason, it is clearly important that these forms of aid be provided in ways that are most beneficial to NDO neighborhood revitalization work and long-term organizational capacity building. This chapter examines the kinds of funding and hands-on technical assistance that may be particularly valuable to NDOs and the reasons such types of aid are useful. Where the limitations of the research, particularly the number of case study sites, allow we also discuss the points in NDO growth at which various forms of assistance are particularly appropriate.

## THE ROLE OF FUNDING

Obviously, NDOs need operating and investment funds to carry out significant community development projects, as well as to survive as organizations conducting programs more generally. As discussed in detail in chapters 2 and 3, because funding is one critical ingredient to successful project development, NDO capabilities that help attract money can be key organizational characteristics. These observations require no further illustration.

In this chapter, we discuss how certain kinds of funding and their creative, strategic use by NDOs can be of special value[1] to NDO success in neighborhood revitalization work. Funding may have impact on organizational survival, the development of key aspects of major projects, the growth of NDO capacities, the raising of other needed funds, or the productivity of funds that are already available. In some instances, funding importance may lie particularly in its timing. In other cases, the general scarcity of funds for particular purposes may enhance their value (or the value of manipulating them effectively).

On the following pages, we discuss some significant types of funding and fund use and the impacts they have on NDO project work in the short and long run. Where possible, we also suggest the role of the timing of funding in relation to NDO project or overall development. Our selection of items for discussion does not imply that other NDO activities could be performed without funds. Instead, the selection provides a focus on types of funding, its timing, and its use, which might be pivotal to NDO progress and involve funds in short supply. These types of funds are potential candidates for expanded assistance from public and private sources and attention from NDOs themselves. The seven aspects of funding we consider are:

---

1. On occasion, funding can be harmful to NDO development. Such instances are also discussed.

- Early funding, before an NDO's track record is established
- Sources of flexible and continuing funds
- Important substitutes for flexible funds
- Major increases in funding scale or scope
- Leveraging funds
- Cycling financial resources within the community
- Project funding levels

Next, we describe each aspect.

### 1. Early Funding, Before an NDO's Track Record is Established

NDOs clearly need modest funds at the outset of their programming efforts in order to hire minimal staff and obtain office space, carry out the planning of initial projects, and support program operations until specific project funding or more major flexible funds can be obtained to provide that support. Many of the criteria that funding sources use to select recipients, such as successful project track records and consistently good homework, simply cannot be demonstrated by NDOs at early stages of work. The willingness of some outside organization to provide funds on the basis of trust, personal impressions of the executive director and perhaps key board members, community roots,[2] or other early, less concrete signs of potential success has been important to each of our 12 sample NDOs. Most of the 12 have received these funds in adequate amounts to get project activity started and build the capacities to obtain other funds and do further work. Principal contributors were churches[3] and certain other local foundations and, less frequently, municipal government. NDOs pointed to those funds as key to early growth. A few of the sample NDOs, as well as many less successful organizations outside our sample, struggle without adequate (or any) start-up money and grow more slowly than if some minimum capacity could be "purchased" early.[4]

### 2. Source of Flexible and Continuing Funds

Continuing funds that can be used flexibly for administration and project development appear very valuable to those few of our sample organizations that obtain them. Lack of such funds causes important parallel difficulties for the others. This finding is highly consistent with those of other observers.

In particular, *flexible* funds allowed hiring good core staff (in advance and at higher salaries than might be possible with project funds); upgrading man-

---

2. Especially for organizations with at least some advocacy history.
3. Both funds and in-kind items such as meeting space.
4. Early funding, as already indicated, also often provides credibility and contacts to establish useful relations with other outsiders.

agement capabilities (in accounting for example); and contracting for helpful, specialized technical assistance. The monies enable organizations to plan and develop future projects—a particular difficulty for those of our organizations most strapped for flexible funds. And general funds allowed NDOs to make needed equity investments in certain projects and to pursue others that they thought were important but which were not priorities of outside funding sources. Each of these elements contributed substantially to the rate at which NDOs could expand their sets of successful revitalization activities.

Adequate flexible monies proved beneficial to NDOs at both advanced and early stages of work. Advanced groups might use the funds to undertake a backlog of projects built upon previous work, to realize their potential to pursue new project types, or to fill specific skill gaps. NDOs at early stages of development might gain such "luxuries" as financial stability while they struggled with early programming, adequate staffing, and opportunities to prepare several projects for simultaneous implementation. Such luxuries contribute significantly to growth.

Substantial *continuing* general funds saved valuable time and effort in fundraising. They helped relieve executive directors' work overloads and attracted staff and other project funders who were concerned with NDO viability.

An important issue is whether having such continuing funds reduces NDO resourcefulness and inhibits diversification of funding sources. If so, continuing funds might leave an organization especially vulnerable to later fund cut offs or to pressures on NDO policy from funding sources. That has not apparently been the pattern for our sample NDOs. The organizations with continuing flexible funds are nonetheless very active in seeking other general and especially project monies and seem explicitly aware and wary of the potential threat posed by single source funding. Indeed, continuing flexible funds have frequently been used to define project opportunities and to prepare proposals for their support from other sources. Because several NDOs in our study have already experienced threatened, planned, or actual cut offs of general funds from a major source, they are probably more alert to the dangers of single source funding than might otherwise be the case.

### 3. Important Substitutes for Flexible Funds

The experiences of our sample NDOs suggest that several types of less flexible funds can effectively play roles which general funds perform when available. In the absence of more flexible funds, these special-purpose monies were often very helpful. One valuable type of funding was for upfront planning and preparation of specific projects. Relatively sophisticated projects in particular required a level of detailed design, prior to implementation, that NDOs found hard to support financially. Only very rarely were funds available specifically for this stage of work, usually as loans for housing projects that allow development costs to be reimbursed from implementation funding. Several NDOs deferred work on projects requiring extensive preparation, cited the need for funds as a reason for slow progress on them, or used general funds they did have for this purpose.

A second useful substitute for flexible general support was funding for timely action on project implementation. Several groups noted that opportunities for projects were lost because funds were not available quickly enough to secure needed land and buildings.[5] In some instances, when NDOs applied (or discussed applying) for funds to carry out projects without having land or buildings in their control, other developers saw the potential of these plans and jumped in ahead of the community organizations. Several NDOs that had flexible funds usable for advance acquisition cited their importance in protecting major project opportunities. Perhaps a revolving fund to NDOs specifically for this purpose could be a useful substitute where general funds are not available.

A third substitute for general funds was financial aid to NDOs when they encountered serious cash flow problems. Several NDOs used short-term loans for operating funds, or forbearance by lenders and investors, to survive crises occasioned by late-paying government contracts or by stalled or financially unsuccessful projects.

Surpluses or profits generated by NDOs' own projects form a final potential substitute for flexible funds from the outside. Generating these profits is a goal of each of our sample organizations. Such funds could be used for any activities NDOs selected. These funds would potentially provide stable, independent support. Not surprisingly, given the difficult conditions under which NDOs operate, surpluses have proved difficult to produce. A significant share of potential surplus-producer projects have, at least in the short run, consumed money and energy. It appears critical to develop these projects carefully in line with NDO internal capacities and the economic potential that the environment provides, so that the projects do not unintentionally become consumers rather than generators of scarce NDO resources.[6]

### 4. Major Increases in Funding Scale or Scope

For several NDOs visited during this study, particular large increases in funding for project-specific or general purposes helped enormously in producing rapid successful programming growth. That is hardly surprising.

---

5. Real estate needed to be tied down either through options or actual purchase. Some NDOs noted that options are not available in their communities.

6. An additional need, related to several of these substitutes for general funds, is for enough project-specific investment funding from government and foundation sources to allow an NDO to establish a track record of project work. As discussed in detail in chapter 2, private lender risk-taking with NDOs often comes very slowly if at all.

More notable is that the NDOs which most successfully took advantage of fund inflow were clearly those which were well-positioned in terms of key capacities discussed previously. Each NDO had a set of existing programs and ideas for programs to serve as the springboard for their expansion, a series of developed internal skills and external relations, and a recognition of gaps to fill by using the new funds. NDOs best taking advantage of fund increases were not necessarily the most advanced of our sample, but ones whose capacities had kept pace with or exceeded their previous funding levels.

Several other NDOs were unable, at least in the short-run, to take substantial advantage of actual or potential major fund additions, such as loan pools, CETA workers, or flexible support, for lack of these capabilities. Most NDOs in this latter group were moving to develop the needed characteristics. But these NDOs were clearly not able to show the rapid expansion of actual project implementation that their better-equipped counterparts demonstrated. Several faced some dissatisfaction from community members or funding sources about the slow pace of delivery of new programs after additional money arrived. A few unsuccessful projects arose from use of funds in ways beyond an NDO's capabilities. This experience shows that, when making funding decisions, both funders and recipients must carefully consider the current capacity of a particular NDO and the speed at which key capabilities can reasonably be developed. The scope and scale of funding need to be matched to the ability to use it.

A related funding problem is the temptation created by available funds. Even very effective NDOs have limits to their speed of growth. But an NDO's success in carrying out projects and developing capacity, as well as the vagaries of government programming, may open many new funding doors at one time. NDOs found it difficult to defer some of these opportunities and to concentrate on institutionalizing current successes, even when many staff and board members felt that limiting growth was an appropriate strategy. Again in these instances, NDOs and funders must exercise restraint and attend seriously to building capacity that will make further NDO expansion feasible in the future.

Increasing total funding and funding stability for NDOs could also help convince the organizations that opportunities can be safely deferred.

### 5. *Leveraging Funds*

In numerous instances, obtaining one initial set of funds was a key catalyst in enabling an NDO to secure other funds for major projects. NDOs used contributions in-hand from neighborhood residents and merchants to attract funding from outside sources, guaranteed private loans with government grants and contracts, and combined numerous small-scale funding sources to finance larger developments. Several increased the willingness of their prime funding source to continue to support them by obtaining new sources of funding as well. And, as mentioned earlier, one organization that lacked minimal funding stability had difficulty securing new project funds from sources concerned about the NDO's ability to survive to project completion.

No simple description identifies the funds that can best be leveraged. What we can conclude is that, for leveraging purposes and other reasons, NDOs benefit from diversified funding; and that funding sources willing to provide the "first" money, or at least willing to make funding commitments conditional on others doing the same, can be especially helpful. We also observed that some of the most advanced, successful NDOs carried out their own leveraging of another kind. They cleverly combined funds available from separate sources for differing purposes—for example, using manpower training resources together with venture loans or grants—to support major projects of substantive interest to their communities.

### 6. Cycling Financial Resources within the Community

As other observers have noted, money newly brought into an NDO's community is most valuable for generating jobs, incomes, and other benefits when it is repeatedly respent there.[7] In addition, money that has historically flowed out of the community can be redirected within by the work of NDOs. Several of our sample organizations, particularly but not only the more advanced ones, were very conscious of this potential and took deliberate account of it in selecting their development strategies. A good example is the effort to develop housing management capability by an NDO that already rehabilitates and constructs housing. Based on the experience of the NDOs we studied, such strategies appear to have substantial potential for increasing the impacts NDOs can make with given levels of outside support.

### 7. Project Funding Levels

The experience of our sample NDOs and experts we interviewed is that NDO projects are regularly underfunded, particularly from government sources. The underfunding causes NDOs substantial difficulties in carrying out programs and often requires them to pour scarce flexible funds into supposedly fully supported projects. Inadequate overhead for supervising CETA activities was cited repeatedly as a prime example.

Many NDOs develop tactics to deal with these problems. Improved advance budgeting, an element of homework described in chapter 2, reduced surprise insufficiencies. Combining CETA workers with other funded programs helped moderate both the CETA overhead drain and the costs of la-

---

7. See, for example, Center for Community Economic Development, "Existing and Alternative Designs for Title VII Programs," Cambridge, Massachusetts, September, 1977.

bor-intensive projects. In one instance, an NDO rehabilitated only part of a building in order to seek additional funds based on that success; and in another an NDO made certain its building tenants decided on the use of available funds, partly in order to limit dissatisfaction with necessarily inadequate services. Both more realistic levels of outside support and further development of such tactics by NDOs can contribute to project successes.

## THE ROLE OF TECHNICAL ASSISTANCE

NDOs have received a wide variety of forms of technical assistance to support their neighborhood revitalization projects and the process of building their own capabilities. Our research has focused on hands-on technical assistance—direct, usually on-site provision of technical services[8] by outside sources. We did not examine off-site training, seminars, workshops, and conferences and written materials such as "how-to" handbooks.

Even within the hands-on category NDOs have used many types of technical assistance. The discussion below focuses on nine types that have been common among our sample NDOs and appear to have been generally beneficial:

- Proposal writing
- Project packaging
- Specialized professional services
- Legal assistance
- Accounting
- Assistance with relations to outsiders, especially funding sources
- Defining board and staff roles and training board members in development
- Organizational design
- Multipurpose project and organizational counsel

The choice is not based on a completely exhaustive compilation of technical assistance received by our sample organizations. NDOs were asked to identify important examples of technical aid, not to catalogue every type of assistance they had ever received.

Our study examines not only common types of useful aid but also the time in an organization's history when various types of technical assistance become particularly valuable. The skills involved in much of the aid can, and it appears often should, be developed in-house as NDOs grow and mature. The discussion below suggests when and sometimes how that internalization might be encouraged to occur. The discussion builds on the concepts of key NDO capabilities and stages in their development that were outlined in chapters 2 and 3. However, the analysis of timing is necessarily restricted. Only

---

8. Including on-site training as well.

a subset of the 12 sample NDOs received any single form of technical assistance and typically some of those NDOs were young. We therefore obtain
limited observations of the process of bringing skills in-house and of technical assistance as an aid or hindrance to it.

Before we examine each type of technical assistance, several broader conclusions warrant discussions. Most important, we found that technical assistance is generally most valuable when an NDO has itself identified, carefully
defined, and contracted for a specific set of technical services. Technical assistance that is used because it is provided free of direct money costs (e.g.,
by a funding source), but without the NDO (or technical assistance group or
funding source) having defined a problem and an approach to dealing with
the problem, often seemed the least useful. Assistance that is sought by the
NDO, but without careful attention to and detailed agreement with the pro-
vider about what technical assistance outputs should be, has also usually
been less successful.

In addition, continuing control over technical assistance is an important
aspect of its successful use. NDOs with the knowledge and confidence to insist throughout that outsiders' performance remain in accord with NDOs'
needs and jointly defined tasks are better able to reap benefits from technical aid.

NDOs appear frequently to have learned the importance of defining and
controlling technical assistance through negative experience. Several mentioned receiving unhelpful assistance in particular project areas and then
later being able to use more clearly defined services in the same area. For
example, an NDO might hire a consultant to investigate overall potential for
commercial revitalization in the NDO's community. This task might be too
general and leave out too many needed components such as contacting key
community actors (e.g., local merchants), to yield any valuable results. But
after an NDO itself learned more about commercial revitalization, the NDO
could hire a new consultant to consider several specific types of possibilities
for projects, to identify next steps in pursuing those projects, and to interact
with community members at specific intervals. All this would be defined in
a detailed contract.

Paying full standard costs of services also frequently improved the value
of technical assistance. Payment seemed to help most specifically by assuring that the work was timely, that the NDO felt comfortable making clear its
needs and demands, and that the NDO worked to make the outside efforts
useful because of its own financial commitment for them.

It is important not to overgeneralize these points. Some free technical assistance, available for general design of strategy and a continually updated
set of tasks, seemed extremely valuable to certain NDOs in early stages of
community development work. A key ingredient in such success may have
been (the sample of experience is very small) special sensitivity by the tech-

nical assistance providers to the possible problems of this less-defined process. The sources of aid worked to help establish objectives for their services and to train NDOs to be able to do that specification in the future.

While much technical assistance was useful, several NDOs received poor quality paid or free assistance that helped lead them into project difficulties. To use technical assistance well, organizations need to develop enough internal understanding of the development process to recognize poor advice. NDOs should have a network of advisors and other means to help examine outsiders' recommendations. Finally, NDOs need the confidence to ask hard questions and make their own decisions.

Discussion of specific uses of technical assistance follows. Of the nine types of assistance discussed, four—aid in proposal writing, project packaging, defining board and staff role, and continuous aid and counsel in early projects—seem perhaps the most broadly valuable to NDOs. But each of the nine played a key role for some of the organizations at various points in project and organizational development.

### 1. Proposal Writing

Three quarters of the NDOs included in this study used substantial technical assistance in proposal writing. While our research could not independently assess the significance of this aid in securing project funding, the NDOs themselves felt that it had played an important role. Many sought it repeatedly from the same sources and reported success in obtaining funds through assisted proposals.

Assistance in proposal writing was clearly most useful for NDOs inexperienced in community development work. These groups frequently lacked what they considered satisfactory in-house skills in project design, project finance, and writing and supplemented those skills from the outside.

In general, NDOs deliberately developed in-house skill in proposal writing as they grew in experience. Often this process took place fairly early in organizational growth. Because many of the needed skills are not too highly specialized, staff members could be trained and/or hired to perform them relatively easily.

Bringing proposal writing skills in-house seems important for NDO capacity development. NDOs and technical assistance providers both felt that independence in proposal writing is an important element of developing NDO resourcefulness. NDOs' flexibility in seeking funds is increased by the NDOs themselves being able to write proposals rather than depending on the availability of aid. And NDOs' understanding of and control over project development is also greatly enhanced by their work in preparing proposals. However, even for more advanced NDOs, occasionally hiring consultants to assist in some highly technical elements of proposal preparation is useful and does not detract from NDO capacity-building.

Most of the sample NDOs that used assistance have been successful in taking over more of their own proposal writing. Successful in-house development involved the commitment of both the technical assistance source and NDO staff to transferring skills as actual proposals were being prepared. Some sources of aid carefully withdrew their participation on a step-by-step basis, offering diminishing consultation and pressing NDOs to do their own design and writing. In other cases, NDOs, understanding the importance of taking over proposal writing, hired staff with appropriate skills, had this staff train others in the organization to assist them, or (in a few cases) obtained formal classroom training. Overall, early technical assistance in proposal writing proved an aid, not a hindrance, to capacity building, if participants gave careful attention to skill transfer.

### 2. Packaging

Many community development projects require "packaging," which includes the preparation of detailed financial and other forms as part of applications for funding, contracting with other investors and participants, and similar activities. Three quarters of our sample NDOs also noted the importance of technical assistance in project packaging: for example, when seeking HUD approval for a subsidized housing project. To a significant extent the NDOs lacked the know-how to perform packaging work themselves and required assistance to move specific projects forward. Again, the aid was most important for younger organizations who were less experienced in development. But in comparison to aid in proposal writing, NDOs needed and used technical assistance in packaging a good deal later in their growth processes. The required knowledge is more highly specialized and technical and thus less likely to be quickly developed in-house.

Several NDOs relied on experienced general contractors or outside development teams to perform the packaging role. As discussed in chapter 2, these participants not only contributed assistance in packaging itself but added to projects' credibility more generally. Other useful packaging aid came from technical assistance organizations who provided a wide range of services to NDOs, including packaging.

Packaging nonetheless seems a task that should be increasingly carried out internally by NDOs. Packaging work by NDOs themselves increases the likelihood that project decisions will be made in the interest of the community rather than of the packagers. It ensures that an NDO can continue project development activity should the packager for some reason sever their relationship. And it allows an NDO to retain a larger share of any development profits.

Several of our more advanced organizations did learn to package their own developments. The processes of developing this skill in-house were similar to the processes used in developing proposal writing skills. In-house development usually required on-the-job training of staff by the source of technical assistance or hiring of staff with packaging experience. A significant difference is that packaging skills are more project-specific than is proposal writing. An NDO could perhaps package its own housing project after having gone through that process with assistance, but the NDO could not easily transfer that experience to another type of project work.

### 3. Specialized Professional Services

Nearly all NDOs, experienced and inexperienced, use consultants for special professional services during project development. Like many private developers, they do not have a sufficient volume of particular types of work to merit keeping certain expensive, professional services in-house. Indeed, advanced organizations may be more frequent users, taking on larger and more complex projects and perhaps better recognizing when they need help.

In our sample, the most frequently used were architectural and engineering services for project building design, real estate agents to investigate and negotiate real estate transactions, and financial consultants to evaluate economic venture alternatives and conduct market studies. Such assistance proved to be more frequently important to physical and economic development than to social service projects. NDOs reported that they generally built service programs themselves, using their own better superior understanding of community needs. However, even social service projects sometimes had unique features that made special technical assistance useful. For example, a major corporation assisted one NDO with its meals-for-senior-citizens program by providing technical assistance in kitchen design, cost control, budgeting, and food preparation.

Some of the specialized skills seem more easily developed in-house than others. In particular, NDOs reported some success in learning to perform their own market studies and analyses of venture financial feasibility, especially at preliminary levels. They then limited their purchases of those skills to consultants with very specific knowledge about the individual economic activities being considered. NDOs did not, on the other hand, try to develop in-house engineering capabilities.

The most important NDO learning process in terms of special services is not internalizing the skills but rather developing the ability to control the consultants. The basic concept of NDO control was discussed at the beginning of this section. However, special professional services pose a particular challenge. Providers frequently do not have significant experience in, or commitment to, dealing effectively with NDOs. They do not automatically work hand-in-hand with NDOs to help structure their work, as do some sources of technical assistance with long histories of involvement with neighborhood organizations. The service providers generally require pressure to perform specific work in line with client needs, just as they do in work for government or private profit sectors. In addition, their skills are so specialized that it is difficult for less-trained NDO staff to oversee the consultants' performance.

NDOs learn by experience to demand clear contracts that specify understandable outcomes and to recognize whether tasks are being properly performed. Partially offsetting the difficulties of control is the fact that the tasks to be undertaken by special services consultants are often inherently quite specific, so that clear definition of what is to be accomplished is relatively easy.

### 4. Legal Assistance

A majority of the NDOs studied deemed technical assistance in legal matters valuable. Common uses were in incorporating an NDO or its spin offs, continued advising on legal powers and limitations of nonprofit corporations, and facilitating real estate transactions or other venture agreements. A few organizations underestimated their needs for such assistance early in their work and encountered unnecessary difficulties—for example, in gaining tax exempt status for their spin offs.

Most NDOs continued to use outside legal help even as they matured. The legal needs of advanced organizations were largely occasional and specialized. Besides working through complex transactions and contracts, legal matters included fighting lawsuits over specific projects and preparing legislation to revise inhibiting local laws. It was therefore logical to buy appropriate legal services instance by instance. A number of NDOs had the advantage of drawing on lawyers formerly active in NDO or related work.

Some NDOs brought legal skills in-house by including attorneys on their boards of directors. This proved an inexpensive and effective way to obtain continuing legal assistance in general organizational deliberations. However, problems sometimes arose when these lawyers had inadequate time and relied too heavily on underprepared NDO staff to carry out their instructions. In addition, major legal tasks were too burdensome to be handled in this manner.

The relatively few NDOs that added lawyers to their permanent staffs usually hired them to pursue some special program-related purpose, for example, to carry on an NDO program of incorporating local towns or to start developing a community-owned law firm. Even these NDOs continued to obtain further outside legal assistance.

### 5. Accounting

Technical assistance made significant contributions to accounting and bookkeeping for many NDOs, at several points in organizational development. Assistance proved important early in NDOs' lives to establish basic manual fund accounting systems, as organizations moved beyond merely having separate checkbooks for each funding source. Many NDOs had no trained bookkeeper on staff as they made the transition from checkbooks to basic accounting systems. They needed outside expertise to develop the means to meet basic financial reporting needs. Board members sometimes provided services on a volunteer basis but were soon overwhelmed by the workload.

Outside accountants established systems to record types of expenses and sources of funds as funding sources required and to yield minimum financial status information to management. Once basic systems were in place, some in-house development of bookkeeping skills commonly occurred. NDOs either trained inexperienced community people or hired new staff. Training often required technical assistance because other staff members frequently had little more accounting knowledge than the trainees.

Newly developed in-house bookkeeping skills enabled NDOs to carry out the established recordkeeping procedures in a timely way, but the organizations frequently needed outside consultation to deal with modestly new or different situations.[9] Differences in reporting requirements among government funding sources occasioned much of this aid as NDOs received new grants and contracts.

Technical assistance continued to be useful as additional complexities or information requirements arose which required changes in the ways records were kept. One repeated example of such a complexity was the need to allocate expenses as NDOs took on projects with multiple funding sources. In a number of instances, board members with accounting or bookkeeping backgrounds were helpful in identifying when further outside assistance should be sought and for what tasks.

As NDOs became sufficiently large and complex to warrant computerization of their accounting tasks, and as their desire grew for more complete and timely financial management information, the organizations made good use of occasional highly sophisticated assistance. A few hired very skilled accountants of their own, trained back-up people, and were able to handle nearly all their accounting matters in-house. Most NDOs gradually added internal capability by training and hiring, but they still relied on outside assistance for new developments. In either case, the services of a respected outside auditor were necessary to protect NDOs from attack by their adversaries and assure meeting funding source guidelines.

Both NDOs and sources of accounting assistance suggested that outside aid was more likely to be successful under two conditions: that the providers not be the NDOs' funding sources and that NDOs be given preliminary counsel and then allowed time to identify their own bookkeeping needs.

---

9. The need for repeated assistance depended heavily on the levels of staff bookkeepers' experience.

## 6. *Assistance with Relations to Outsiders, Especially Funding Sources*

A smaller number of NDOs emphasized the usefulness of technical assistance in helping them make early contacts with key actors in government, foundations, and private business. The assistance generally came from sources highly experienced in working with NDOs. The aid was most valuable soon after an NDO had raised its first project monies and begun project activities.

Providers of this assistance helped to identify potential funding sources and specific individuals to contact within them. They advised on strategy (types of projects likely to be supported) and tactics (key ideas to emphasize in presentation, even clothes to wear). In some instances, sources of technical aid directly arranged contacts between NDO executive directors and business leaders and government officials. They also advised NDOs on where to find potential friends among these groups.

In all of this work, the key is to transfer knowledge and skill *quickly* to the NDO itself. The transfer is principally to the executive director, who gains tools to support his/her own resourcefulness and entrepreneurial talent. The technical assistance must then soon be withdrawn, to assure independent NDO action in developing its external relations. According to experts we interviewed, however, such guidance can neither substitute for nor create entrepreneurship capabilities if the executive director, and/or perhaps another key staffer, does not have the basic talent and inclination.

## 7. *Defining Board and Staff Roles and Training Board Members in Development*

Many NDO staff and board members felt that outside assistance was very valuable in working out the roles that board and staff members should play, though only half the study NDOs actually had employed such aid. They believed that "neutral" outsiders could serve several functions because of their lack of direct involvement.

Sources of technical assistance could speak from experience about the ways other NDOs had successfully allocated responsibilities. The sources could suggest approaches that might appear to be power grabbing if they came from one group of the direct participants. Outsiders could recognize instances of misunderstanding and lack of communication that more directly involved NDO participants interpreted as firm disagreement. Trained facilitators could then encourage board and staff to discuss their respective problems—a practice that allowed each to see the other as seeking authority in order to meet organizational objectives, rather than for the sake of control. And outsiders could help identify and define consensus positions and convert them into written agreements, rules, and policies. Sources of assistance that helped bring about specific straightforward discussions, rather than using complex techniques of "organizational dynamics," and that had specific experience with NDOs, were particularly helpful.

Technical assistance on board/staff role definition was particularly valuable when intensive disagreement occurred between the two groups. As discussed earlier, these disagreements might occur at quite different points in organizational life history. And they may even recur, especially after substantial turnover of board and/or staff.

Technical assistance in developing procedures for hiring and firing staff, however, was far more useful before crises occurred. During consideration of specific, controversial personnel cases, NDO participants' feelings about the individuals to be hired or fired were often too strong to allow new procedures to be created and properly carried out.

Technical assistance designed to increase board members' understanding of community development projects and processes could also contribute to the effectiveness of the board in policymaking and oversight. The aid was most important when NDOs first moved into development, but recurrent efforts were needed as board members and projects changed. NDOs and experts felt, however, that this service could be equally well performed in-house by staff and technically trained board members. In either case, training usually seemed more successful when presented as part of the process of examining real NDO projects, rather than in considering "development in the abstract." Board members' interest was then much higher and their time not stretched as thin by separate meetings for decision making and for training.

### 8. Organizational Design

One third of the NDOs studied mentioned technical assistance in structuring their organizations as being valuable in several ways. The use of aid most often mentioned is in determining appropriate composition of the board of directors. Boards of directors can perform very different primary roles in different NDOs—support building in the community, policymaking, technical counsel, political contact—depending on the overall needs and the availability of other resources to the NDO. The assistance of an outsider was sometimes useful in clarifying what an NDO hoped to accomplish through its board and analyzing how board membership should be distributed to meet those objectives. Other related types of aid include help in design of the ways board responsibilities are shared (e.g., committee structure), staff functions are centralized or decentralized, coalitions are structured, and "parent" organizations relate to their spin offs (e.g., interlocking boards).

Technical assistance in organizational design is clearly most appropriate at the inception of the NDO, or when project needs and/or resources merit the establishment of an affiliated organization.

### 9. Multipurpose Project and Organizational Counsel

#### a. Detailed planning, design, and implementation

For a few of our study NDOs, sources of technical assistance provided continuous aid and counsel through all stages of development of their early projects. The assistance included help in proposal writing and packaging as just discussed. But aid in those specific forms was part of a more complete set of services that also included detailed involvement in strategy development, project selection, planning, design, and implementation. The technical assistance providers helped identify the steps in the development process and then helped carry out these steps.

Based on a very small sample of experience, high quality, detailed technical assistance of this type appeared very valuable in moving early projects along while NDOs developed their own capabilities. Projects that might have had to be deferred, or that might have proceeded only very slowly as new problems and situations were encountered, were able to continue more smoothly. A track record was thus established more quickly. On the other hand, one study organization was hurt by what turned out to be a poor quality of assistance. That NDO's experience represents an important danger for NDOs who lean heavily on continuous outside aid but are not skilled in assessing its quality.

It is critical that NDOs work actively, with the cooperation of their sources of continuous, detailed assistance, to internalize the basic capabilities necessary for carrying out projects. The skills of project implementation especially need to be transferred to NDOs (and/or hired internally by them) at an early stage. The day-to-day problems of managing rehabilitation of houses, for example, are simply too numerous to depend on even quite frequently available technical assistance. The other skills that sources of continuous technical assistance contribute obviously form many of the capabilities fundamental to independent neighborhood revitalization work. If the NDOs are to develop real capacity of their own, this kind of assistance must contribute to rather than substitute for the process of internalizing skills.

It is difficult to tell how continuous, multifaceted technical assistance is affecting internalization for the very small set of organizations we observed who were receiving this aid, especially since these NDOs are in general still young organizations. Our best judgment is that where technical assistance providers and NDOs are conscious of the need to create independent capability, extensive assistance need not interfere with and may contribute to that process.

#### b. General counsel

Unlike the *continuous* technical assistance just discussed, general counseling is a *continuing* form of more occasional aid that has proved valuable to several sample NDOs. It is focused not solely on early stages of an NDO's development but rather provides the NDO with feedback throughout its lifetime.

In our experience, trusted, long-term sources of technical assistance have been useful in discussing appropriate strategies and programs for pursuing NDO goals, identifying needs for further capacity building, and recognizing external constraints and opportunities. These sources sometimes help encourage NDOs to step back to assess past achievements and plan future directions. They may provide executive directors the opportunity to discuss problems that the directors prefer not to share with board, staff, community, or funding sources. For this reason, experts and NDOs suggest that such aid is best not tied to a funding source.

## Summary of the Role of Technical Assistance

In sum, technical assistance of numerous types can be systematically valuable to NDOs. Just how useful it is, in moving projects forward and especially in building NDO capacity over the long term, depends on several characteristics of its delivery. Many types of aid need to be provided early in the process of an NDO's development, but such aid must fill in for undeveloped internal skills without conflicting with internal maturation. For best results, both NDO participants and providers of technical assistance need to work consciously to transfer skills to the neighborhood organization's staff (and in some instances board) in the course of gaining their immediate benefits. And for both assistance at early stages and specialized services delivered later in organizations' growth processes, NDOs must carefully and insistently define, manage, and control outside technical aid to meet their needs.

# V. PERFORMANCE MEASURES

We are interested in measuring the performance of NDOs in developing and implementing revitalization projects for at least two broad reasons. First, we may want to assess how productive the resources devoted to supporting NDO projects are relative to their value in potential alternative neighborhood revitalization uses. Second, we may want to compare the performance of different NDOs. That second comparison could help analyze both what types of NDOs will use resources effectively and might therefore receive priority for funding and what elements of capacity we should help NDOs to build. Because of the importance of these objectives, given the scarcity of aid availability to NDOs, this chapter examines in some detail how NDO project performance can properly be measured.

A wide variety of strategies might be used to measure NDOs' performance. The precise purpose for which performance is being measured should play an important role in determining what strategy is selected. For example, two studies[1] of CSA's Title VII-funded Community Development Corporations (CDCs) were intended to examine the impacts of the whole range of CDC activities, in terms of the long list of stated objectives of that federal program and of the organizations themselves. Researchers therefore needed to develop and use a large number of essentially equally weighted measures, which corresponded to these objectives and to the multiple programs CDCs operated in pursuit of them. On the other hand, in The Urban Institute's analysis of Ford Foundation-funded CDCs,[2] researchers, funders, and CDCs all agreed early in the process on a narrower focus. Development of performance measures concentrated on quantifying direct economic and physical outputs of projects and comparing them to established goals.

We discuss performance measures here in terms of their usefulness in examining the results of assistance to NDOs under HUD's Neighborhood Self-Help Development program (NSHD) or similar programs. The NSHD program has two major goals:

1. To provide grants and other assistance to neighborhood organizations to undertake housing economic development, community development, and other neighborhood conservation and revitalization projects in low and moderate-income neighborhoods; and

2. To increase the capacity of neighborhood organizations to carry out

---

1. Abt Associates, "Evaluation of the Special Impact Program," 1972, and Center for Community Economic Development (CCED), "Existing and Alternative Designs for Title VII Programs," Cambridge, Massachusetts, September 1977.

2. Harvey Garn, Nancy Tevis, and Carl Snead, "Evaluating Community Development Corporations—A Summary Report," The Urban Institute, Washington, D. C., March 1976.

such revitalization projects using and coordinating other resources from private and public sectors and the neighborhood itself.

Our principal objectives in designing means to assess NDO performance, therefore, are to measure success in (1) implementing specific neighborhood revitalization projects and (2) developing NDO capacities for similar future work.

Two caveats are appropriate. First, we do not attempt to establish specific measures for impacts of every potential project or changes in every key characteristic of capacity. Instead, we illustrate concepts and provide examples. Second, we do not specifically focus on outputs of projects' planning processes—for example, the quality of final specifications or funding-application packages for a housing project—that are part of the NSHD program's focus, but only on those of project implementation itself.

The discussion below describes, in conceptual terms and with examples, an approach to measuring NDO project impacts and capacity building. It focuses first on primary, direct, easily visible project outputs. We examine how they might be measured and compared to internal and, where appropriate, external standards. We then explain how these simple measures need to be modified, to take into account equity issues—the distribution of project benefits and costs—and the level of difficulty created by an NDO's environment.

The presentation next turns to measurement of a series of impacts of NSHD-type assistance other than primary direct project results. These include less primary but still direct outputs (e.g., jobs in a housing rehabilitation project), indirect impacts (actions by other parties in response to NDO project activity), and NDO capacity building. Such impacts are as significant to evaluation of total program costs and benefits as are primary direct outputs, but the discussion of their measurement can be shortened by reference to issues raised in the previous discussion of primary direct effects.

Finally, we consider a small set of issues that have been of special concern in similar impact measurement efforts. The three main issues are treatment of leveraging and self-help, consideration of NDO project impact on communitywide outcomes (e.g., on the neighborhood's overall unemployment rate), and assessment of the importance and value of particular projects to the community.

## PRIMARY DIRECT "PHYSICAL" OUTPUTS

The focus of our effort to design performance measures is on impacts of specific NDO projects seen as means to revitalize neighborhoods. Therefore, we concentrate first on measurement of the primary direct results of a given project for its neighborhood. Identifying the one or two direct objectives of an NDO effort should generally be a straightforward process. A housing rehabilitation project may well have a single primary objective: completing renovation of a set of dwelling units. An NDO's project of building an industrial facility and leasing it to a private firm that agrees to hire workers from the organization's manpower program has two primary direct objectives: (1) completing the building and (2) actually securing the employment.

One significant difference from past overall evaluations of CDCs is that earning profits from a venture, which an NDO might have as a high priority objective, would generally be treated separately from key direct outputs. The reason is that profit making is not itself an element of neighborhood revitalization. Profit earning would better be labeled, for these purposes, an element of capacity building (a subject to which we shall return), as well as an indicator of whether direct venture outputs such as employment or building repair can be sustained in the longer term.

Standard measures of the number, size or other scale of the direct outputs; their costs per unit; and time elapsed per unit could be used as simple indicators of the extent and efficiency of accomplishment. Specifics about the unit of output would have to be recorded, in most instances, to make accurate cost comparisons possible. For example, the extent of the renovation being undertaken in a given dwelling will affect cost and should certainly be controlled for in measuring it.

The length of time over which performance can be evaluated will have important impacts on the quality of measurement. Getting apartment buildings fully rented, job slots completely filled, or ventures to intended levels of production of goods and services (and profits) may take substantial time. Ultimate performance may be only poorly predicted by immediate results.

The absolute measures of output just discussed can be made more meaningful by examining outputs relative to established standards as well. Basic output measures could properly be compared to two kinds of standards to judge direct output performance. The first type of comparison is to the level of direct accomplishments originally proposed by an NDO. Sources of assistance are presumably providing aid because they consider promised results worth their investment. Total results (direct and other less immediate) no doubt depend heavily on delivery of primary direct outputs, and assistance sources may place heavy weight on the primary direct outputs themselves because of their clear linkages to NDO action. Therefore, achieving proposed primary outputs is a central measure of achieving overall promised results.[3] NDOs should not be expected to match predicted performance exactly but to come within margins of error experienced by others doing similar work.

---

3. In addition, ability to predict accurately what can be accomplished has proved to be a fairly important element of capability for future success: especially to attract funding and to avoid budgetary difficulties.

A second appropriate comparison is between NDO performance and the unit cost and time experience of other actors carrying out similar activities. This type of comparison is important because outputs originally proposed by NDOs may in fact represent widely varying levels of accomplishment. Comparison could be made to the past work of the NDO itself, to work by others in the same or similar circumstances or locations, and/or to a more "outside" but more readily available standard for similar activity. The first two possibilities better reflect the difficulties encountered in a specific project that are beyond NDO control. But the first standard also could reflect past NDO weaknesses, so that we may to some extent be measuring capacity growth rather than solely current effectiveness.

On the other hand, genuinely comparable outside (non-NDO) experience may be very difficult to find. Private and even public actors may have chosen not to attempt similar project work under conditions similar to those NDOs frequently face. As a result, directly comparable efforts may not exist. Efficiency comparisons with similar projects undertaken under far different conditions may primarily reflect the differences in circumstances rather than differences in real performance. This inaccuracy of comparison may persist even when efforts like those discussed next are made to take into account the level of environmental difficulty. In a perhaps significant set of cases, the problems may be so great that numerical comparisons with work by actors outside the NDO or NDO neighborhood will be inappropriate.

Another significant point in comparing NDO performance with that of other projects is that comparability must not be limited to primary direct outputs. NDO projects, in general and under programs such as NSHD in particular, will often by design produce other impacts (e.g., hiring neighborhood youths, building NDO capacity for future work) that are valuable and require time and money. Such beneficial impacts may well not result from private sector efforts that have the same primary direct objectives. Any measuring of comparability must take into account variations in the full range of benefits that are produced by project work. Benefits other than primary direct outputs are discussed in this chapter under "Other Impacts."

A final key aspect of measuring primary direct outputs is analysis of the *distribution of benefits* to groups of people. NSHD and other similar programs intend that direct (and indirect) benefits go to low and moderate income people within an NDO's neighborhood. Primary outputs must therefore be enumerated by beneficiary if measurements are to represent program objectives meaningfully. Including measurement of benefit distribution is also a way to handle certain problems that arise in comparing costs of projects. In particular, larger costs might be incurred to aid more severely deprived people. For example, an NDO housing rehabilitation program may spend money to write down the cost of houses it buys to repair and resell, in order to reach poorer potential owners. Proper performance evaluation should compensate for the added expense associated with such efforts.

## LEVEL OF DIFFICULTY

In general, NDOs are carrying out their activities under circumstances that make project development difficult and may well have discouraged other actors (private and public) from even attempting similar actions. These circumstances must be taken into account when assessing NDOs' outputs and suggesting the importance of NDOs' activities for their communities.

Conceptually, the impacts of environmental conditions can be represented very simply in terms of an economic production function. Suppose an NDO wishes to produce an output Y and has its own inputs I (staff skills, management organization, etc.) to combine with outside aid O. Suppose that conditions of the NDO's environment E are in particular such that vandalism losses for any project are high, political clout of the neighborhood is too low to get quick city action on needed regulatory approvals, and private lenders will not lend under any circumstances. E serves as a series of parameters of the production function that affect how much Y can be produced from given I and O.

$$Y = f (I, O; E)$$

This notion has been discussed recently in a CDC context by Tracy.[4] But he limits his attention to environmental factors that must be present in adequate amount to "absorb" infusions of capital (through CDCs) into the community: for example, adequate skilled labor. Our concept is necessarily broader. It encompasses a wider range of constraints imposed by the environment and relations to outsiders, unchangeable at least in the short run, that affect the ability of NDOs to carry out projects with given internal resources. The external constraints and advantages differ in type and intensity among NDOs, and between NDOs and other actors carrying out similar activities in other locations. They therefore must be measured with care, in order to interpret measured NDO project productivity.

Key NDO characteristics discussed in chapter 2—principally the environmental characteristics and secondarily the relations-to-outsiders—suggest the major parameters of difficulty or advantage that may need to be measured. Some, mainly cost items such as high land prices or energy needs in particular locations, are easy to measure directly. Many of these should be dealt with by initially establishing proper comparative project standards and by having proper bases of cost for similar projects.

Most measurement of external conditions is more elusive. A promising

4. Brian Tracy, "Developing a Capacity-Performance Model for Community Development Corporations," CCED Newsletter, Cambridge, Massachusetts, Winter 1979.

means to assess a number of other conditions is to measure the level of activity, similar to the NDO project, that has occurred in the recent past without NDO action. The activity could be measured absolutely or in comparison to NDO current activity or activity in other neighborhoods. For example, the difficulty of obtaining uninsured loans may be fairly well proxied by levels of recent lender activity in a neighborhood.[5] Or the difficulty of convincing neighborhood homeowners to work with an NDO to rehabilitate their homes may be measured by their private repair expenditures or participation in city-run programs. If performance measures for a large sample of NDOs were assembled along with such measures of difficulty, multivariate statistical techniques might allow the importance of individual constraints to be quantified; but the number of factors is so large that a very substantial set of observations would be required.[6]

In addition to the categories of difficulties suggested in chapter 2 above, NDOs may experience special but unique difficulties in the course of program implementation. An example we actually encountered was a major arson in recently rehabilitated housing. Our experience with NDO recordkeeping suggests that these problems are frequently not documented on a systematic and accessible basis unless the project funding source insists that delays and extra costs be explained in writing. Thus for these difficulties to be measured and taken into account, most NDOs will have to be specifically requested by a funding source to identify them in writing as they occur. This recording would enable observers to assess their significance on a case-by-case basis.

## OTHER IMPACTS

Projects carried out by NDOs often have at least three kinds of effects in addition to primary direct outputs. These include other direct outputs, indirect impacts, and capacity-building impacts. Not all are necessarily measures of NDO performance alone. From the viewpoint of evaluating the total effectiveness of aid to NDOs for their projects, however, they must be included among benefits (or costs as appropriate). For public policies and programs such as NSHD, designed broadly to support neighborhood revitalization efforts, these other impacts are no less important than primary direct outputs.

We discuss measurement of each of these additional types of impacts be-

---

5. Private lender uninsured financing as compared to all financing for similar purposes in the area may be the desired measure more specifically.

6. Abt Associates attacked this problem using factor analysis to reduce the number of independent variables in their study of CDCs. The information lost about individual characteristics is quite substantial (See Abt Associates, "Special Impact Program," Vol. II, chapters 3.7.1 and 6.4.3).

low. Three issues just considered under primary direct outputs—namely, the importance of considering (1) NDO project's full range of impacts in making comparison to non-NDO projects; (2) the distribution of project costs and benefits, and (3) the project difficulties imposed by environmental conditions—apply to each of other direct outputs, indirect impacts, and capacity-building impacts as well. We do not separately repeat discussion of those issues. The three additional types of impacts of interest are as follows:

## 1. Other Direct Outputs

And NDO projects generally have other immediately attributable direct results beyond their primary objectives. One example is employing neighborhood residents in the course of a housing rehabilitation project (for which housing improvement is the primary goal). Number of jobs and wages could be measured in the same ways used for measuring direct primary outputs. The other elements of measurement—cost or time per unit, comparisons to projections and standards, and distribution of benefits—would again be appropriate. Similar types of problems, such as time lags, would again have to be considered.

Purchases from local businesses and employment training for area residents, in the process of carrying out development projects, are other examples of direct but nonprimary benefits from projects. Demolition of housing on a new construction site, or falling sales by local businesses competing with NDO ventures, represent losses of a parallel type. Deliberate actions to create added benefits or to avoid the losses—to support neighborhood merchants, train the unemployed or avoid demolitions or destructive competition—might involve extra costs in time and money. The benefits (reduced losses) from these actions should be counted in explaining any excesses of NDO project costs over the standards set by the experience of other actors.[7]

## 2. Indirect Impacts

Other people will probably take actions in response to the project activities of NDOs. In many cases, generating these actions by a community's members may be an important NDO objective in undertaking a project in the first place. A straightforward example is increased home maintenance and repair by neighbors after an NDO rehabilitates the investment-discouraging, "eyesore" homes on a block.

From a narrow point of view, these responses are largely not specifically measures of NDO performance. An NDO may conduct all of its rehabilitation work efficiently, successfully train and employ many people, and aid

---

7. Assuming the other actors have not provided these same direct nonprimary benefits (or minimized the project-related losses).

those genuinely in need. Still, external conditions (e.g., resident incomes) may not permit much secondary impact. The NDO may have little control over indirect responses.

From a somewhat broader viewpoint, we could consider indirect impacts that NDOs described in advance as expected results from their projects to be an element of performance. An NDO's ability to identify projects that do produce useful secondary responses, given the neighborhood environment, and to identify the tasks needed to achieve such responses would be the specific elements of performance under consideration.[8]

In either case, from the viewpoint of evaluating a *program* of assistance to NDOs, we must include these indirect impacts in measurements of benefits (and costs). Two substantial difficulties are apparent. The first is the problem of attribution of impacts. How big a share of increased private rehabilitation can be said to be the result of NDO project activity, given a host of other changes that may have occurred in a neighborhood in the same period? The usual complex problems of obtaining adequate models of behavior, control neighborhoods, or other types of controls for diverse NDO projects arise. Second is the problem of time period of measurement. Indirect impacts may occur only significantly after NDO projects are completed. If program evaluation extends only to project completion or shortly beyond, many indirect impacts may be missed. Timing an evaluation to extend beyond the immediate implementation period for at least some of the projects under examination may be helpful in identifying indirect benefits generated by particular projects.

Finally, multiplier effects are an indirect impact of interest for any kind of NDO project. Resources brought into a community from the outside for a project will in part circulate within the neighborhood and create additional jobs, incomes, and other benefits. And these may well be resources that would not otherwise enter the kinds of neighborhoods in which NDOs operate. Their impacts are relevant only in a very limited way to NDO performance measurement. In the main, multipliers are outside NDO control, though in some instances NDO project selection may help produce high multipliers. But multiplier effects are systematically relevant to an evaluation of total project benefits.[9]

Unfortunately, tracking these payments in specific cases is an enormous undertaking. Previous CDC evaluations have for that reason neglected the issue. Other approaches might be to try to estimate the community multiplier for one or two neighborhoods as a beginning approximation, and to try to

---

8. If an NDO took actions such as educational outreach, or linkages to lenders for neighborhood residents not in the homes the NDO itself repaired, responses would be direct rather than indirect impacts.

9. That is, so long as our focus is on benefits to particular neighborhoods, from resources that can be identified as entering the neighborhoods only as a result of project efforts.

uncover the occasional local, often unpublished research that has addressed local multiplier measurement.

### 3. Capacity Building

A major goal of the Neighborhood Self-Help Development program and of other programs of assistance to NDOs is to increase the organizations' management and programmatic capacity to undertake future projects. Assessing how well NDOs have been able to use aid to increase their capabilities is thus an important, though difficult, element of measuring NDO performance and evaluating aid program benefits. With care, that assessment can be made concrete, specific, and measurable.

The first step in measuring capacity building is to identify the aspects of capacity that are important enough to successful revitalization work to warrant close attention. The findings of this study regarding key characteristics constitute one careful effort at that identification. A number of internal characteristics (described in chapter 2) and relations to outsiders (chapter 2 and chapter 4) may well be significantly affected by NDO work that uses NSHD or similar aid. Resulting changes in development of these elements of capacity should be analyzed. Environmental characteristics, on the other hand, probably will be affected little by a single project.[10] They are more appropriately the focus in measuring difficulties and constraints NDOs face that are beyond their control than items for attention in capacity building.

The other major and difficult step in evaluating capacity building is actually measuring changes in given NDO capabilities. In rare instances, quantification is fairly straight forward. For example, one way to obtain a continuing source of flexible funds for general purposes or venture development (identified above as a key characteristic) is to establish a profitable business (say with NSHD aid). New profits, granted the aforementioned problem of short-term versus long-term results, can clearly by "counted," as can a baseline of past profits (or total flexible funds) to reflect the importance of this new source.

An intermediate case is, for example, participation by an experienced private development group with the NDO on a project. The baseline of whether such cooperation has occurred in the past should be readily discernible, and whether it occurs in a NSHD-supported project should be obvious. Less apparent is the future productivity of new relationships. Have the private groups and the NDO found the relationship positive enough to continue? Do outsiders view the results of their teamwork highly enough to attract future capital?[11] We would need to answer such questions by interviewing relevant

---

10. Possible exceptions are projects that are large scale and/or highly localized.

11. We neglect here the impenetrable issue of whether the NDO would have developed the same relationship without NSHD assistance.

parties about them and by examining direct outputs and problems of the current project, unless study continued long enough to examine future developments directly.

Most key characteristics are fundamentally more difficult to measure. Often evaluators could obtain relatively crude proxies and use them from a distance, for purposes of assuring diversity among a sample of NDOs chosen to be included in an evaluation. But measuring actual capacity development resulting from project work is far more delicate. A primary task in that process is to pinpoint what specific elements of a broadly designated element of capacity are most important and to pursue those.

Consider for example an NDO's need for a staff member qualified and experienced in community development projects, a need which we have previously identified as crucial to project success. Simply to select NDO sites for study, resumes of key project staff people and indications of which technical skills will be provided by outsiders should be adequate to assure some diversity. But to measure in detail what skills and experience are *developed* by a particular NDO staff during (as a result of) a supported project effort requires more careful means. In some cases, a project may allow an experienced staff member to be hired where none with a similar role or qualifications existed. In such instances, the additions to the NDO's technical skills are relatively apparent from a resume and may be pinpointed further by interviewing. Even then, information on whether the new staff person can be retained after the project is complete, and whether (s)he puts technical skills to work with sensitivity to community objectives, would have to be obtained by direct contact with various NDO participants.

In some other cases, the potential key development staffer may already be present; but (s)he may need to gain additional skills and experience. Checking whether the staff person has any past experience with the type of project to be aided is only a beginning. Roles the person played and learning actually gained during project development may vary widely. Measuring capacity building requires baseline interviews with the staff member and knowledgeable outsiders who have worked with him or her. Our research indicates that the key points for interview investigation include how well the staffer understands what steps go into project development, which steps (s)he has actually carried out, and how substantial her/his sense is of the way this project both fits with past NDO development efforts and can lead to future projects. Repeated interviews on these issues with the staffer and with outsiders working on the project, along with documentation of staff participation in particular tasks, should provide evidence of progress. A further item of interest (regardless of whether the lead staff is recruited or trained) is the extent to which current development processes are also being used to train back-up staff.

The mechanisms we suggest for studying growth in staff capabilities (or similar capacity building) differ notably from those used in some past efforts at evaluation. In Abt's work, for example, interviewers asked individuals whether or not their project management skills had increased in the course of the Special Impact program and noted the share of positive responses.[12] Emphasis was on the benefits of NDO experience to those individuals. To identify impacts on capacity for the NDO as an *organization* we must address more specific elements of capacity development, even where quantitative measurement is inexact or intractable. To do this effectively, we narrow the set of relevant elements of capacity and then concentrate on measuring their specific changes. Our increased understanding of what affects NDO success[13] and of how capacities grow[14] should help shape this measurement.

For some other key characteristics, several quantitative measures may exist. But it may be unclear which, if any, usefully proxy the substance of the characteristic. For example, community roots may be quantified by numbers of participants in "actions," annual meetings, or volunteer projects; numbers of members; or numbers of program recipients. Our experience is that on-site interviewing can help indicate which of these should serve as the proxy by indicating which element of community roots is relevant to organizational needs. For example, observers inside and outside one organization identified the involvement of existing block clubs (as members) in NDO activities as a key to expanded housing rehabilitation and other neighborhood programming. The appropriate proxy, block club membership in the NDO in our example, can then be specifically observed during the course of the project. With such initial identification of the elements that really matter, quantitative proxies for roots could be used, along with before-and-after project surveys of residents' knowledge and approval of NDO activities, to signal growth in community support. Again, the lessons of previous chapters can guide this process.

As indicated earlier, we make no attempt here to offer measurements of growth in each key characteristic. Three main points should be recognized in their development. First, capacity growth is a central but difficult part of performance measurement and evaluation for programs such as NSHD and related forms of aid to NDOs. It deserves and requires extensive, careful treatment. Second, identifying a set of capacities and growth processes to examine is a significant limiting step to which previous sections of this paper contribute. Third, for a given characteristic of capacity, measurement should follow from an understanding of the specific aspects of it that have proven important to an NDO's success, although these aspects may not be the easiest to quantify.

---

12. Abt Associates, "Special Impact Program," chapter 4.3.

13. Chapters 2 and 4.

14. Chapter 3.

# FURTHER CONSIDERATIONS IN PERFORMANCE MEASUREMENT

Several other aspects of NDO performance measurement deserve attention as follows:

## 1. Leveraging and Community Self-Help

From the point of view of measuring general NDO performance, disregarding any program evaluation intent, the extent to which one pot of funds is used to leverage another is not necessarily a key separate component. Without a focus on results of a particular program, it is often unclear which funds are leveraging and which being leveraged, where multiple sources are necessary to finance a single project. The ability to bring resources together is reflected in the scale of an NDO's direct project accomplishments and, on the capacity-building side, in improved relationships with funders.

However, from the perspective of evaluating NSHD-type programs, one would be very much interested in the amount of other resources the project grants helped bring together (per grant dollar). Leveraging is both a legislative goal (building capacity to coordinate resources) and a grantee selection criterion, and getting larger scale accomplishments for given dollars is an obvious objective.

Measurement of leveraging is straightforward for commitments of funds. Potentially, consideration may be given separately to private and public funds leveraged perhaps to non-riskfree (not guaranteed, insured) private investments which our investigations suggest are uncommon.[15] Technical assistance and other types of resources leveraged may be either dollar-quantified or listed separately. Because projects may to some extent be selected for aid because of their leveraging level in the first place, it would also be useful to compare expected to actual leveraging accomplished.

The same conceptual points apply to separate measurement of community self help. In narrow NDO performance measurement terms, the self help an NDO obtains might be seen as an element of total project delivery and capacity building. But it is in fact also an important objective of NSHD and many other forms of NDO assistance. In practice, measurement may be somewhat difficult to define in a single index, depending on what activities are included and how varied people's skills and contributions are. Dollar valuation can be used to the extent that volunteer labor substitutes for work often performed in the marketplace.

---

15. Again, we do not believe determining whether projects would have been assembled without HUD aid is feasible.

## 2. Community Outcomes

Observers have often debated whether to consider changes in broad community conditions as implicit measures of NDO performance. Should neighborhoods' rates of housing deficiency, unemployment levels, or feelings of empowerment—once NDO work is undertaken—be considered in assessing NDO success? One major argument for this inclusion is that NDOs often set improving these conditions as organizational objectives. Another is that some programs, namely Title VII's Special Impact program, are broadly and continuously supportive of the whole range of an NDO's efforts to accomplish those goals. The contrary view holds that an NDO should be accountable only for its success in improving conditions over what they would otherwise be, and not be held accountable for the impacts of numerous factors beyond its control that may dominate the determination of community outcomes.

We believe that at least for a program such as the project-specific grants under NSHD, community outcomes should not be a focus of measurement. The scope and intent of one-project support is too narrow to expect NDOs to fundamentally change the direction of neighborhood conditions as a program result. Environmental forces will necessarily still be playing a substantial determining role rather than becoming endogenous. Furthermore, evaluation timing will likely be project oriented, without the opportunity to reflect on long periods of past programming as in the evaluation of CSA's Special Impact program. In addition, separating the role of NSHD-supported projects from other simultaneous NDO activities would often be infeasible.

Instead, the direct and, where possible, indirect impacts of supported NDO projects on the variables which describe community conditions should be measured as we have just outlined. That analysis separates the effects of specific NDO work from those of environmental conditions and other actors' activities. Separation of that kind seems to be the appropriate structure for such a program evaluation. Direct measurement is also methodologically far more tractible than starting with community outcomes and trying to separate out the roles of various contributors to them.[16] Measures of community conditions *could* be used as base points to reflect, in comparison to scale of NDO activity, how substantial a portion of a community problem the organization is able to address.

## 3. Importance of Projects to the Community

The importance of an NDO's project to its community may be worth separate measure. This measure would reflect the NDO's responsiveness to

---

16. CCED's "Existing and Alternative Designs for Title VII Programs, volume III, Performance Measures," (September 1977) inexplicably takes the opposite view on ease of methodology.

community needs[17] and ability to select projects accordingly and would provide an implicit weighting of project benefits. Appropriate measures could include a survey of resident priorities, examination of resident support efforts in its behalf, or data on the intensity of the problem addressed.[18]

Projects may be important to a community for reasons other than that they serve high priority, immediate needs. Instead (or in addition) a project may be significant because it contributes to a broader revitalization strategy that has the long-run potential to make major improvements in neighborhood conditions. In performance measurement efforts less focused on specific projects, assessing the quality of an NDO's revitalization strategy and the usefulness of projects in forwarding a promising strategy could be critical elements of evaluation. Such evaluation requires a broad look at the community impact of various possible approaches by an NDO to revitalizing its neighborhood and is beyond the scope of this project-centered discussion.

## SUMMARY

In sum, even after we narrow the purposes for which we are measuring NDO performance, we need many measures of success to present a complete evaluation. In examining the results of an NDO assistance program such as NSHD, we are concerned with an extended series of direct project outputs, indirect neighborhood revitalization impacts, and effects on NDOs' own capabilities. In the first two of these areas of measurement, we must also consider the range, distribution, and importance of project benefits and the environmental constraints under which they are developed. And in all three areas, but especially that of capacity building, we confront very difficult technical problems of measurement. Increased understanding of the processes of NDO development—the subject of this paper—and of neighborhood revitalization more generally is a vital component of designing adequate means of NDO performance measurement and program evaluation.

---

17. Especially since NSHDA offers responsiveness to community as a primary reason for supporting NDO efforts.

18. See Carl Snead, "On the Need for A Set of Community Weights for Community Development Corporations," The Urban Institute, Washington, D.C., 1974, for a description of this device as a proxy for benefit weights.

# APPENDIX A

## Study Methods

The principal research means for meeting our study objectives were a review of existing literature, interviews with recognized experts in NDO activity and development, and site visits to 12 NDOs. The literature review and expert interviews served primarily to help establish hypotheses for study in the field work. We developed a set of potential key characteristics for success based on information from those sources. We also identified potentially important types of outside assistance and related issues of the proper timing of aid. From these hypotheses, we then prepared interview guides for use at the 12 NDO field sites.

NDOs chosen for case study represent diversity along a number of dimensions. One set of variables we used to select the sample is a series of seven scenarios about organizational growth and development. The purpose of using them was to obtain a spectrum of what might represent important stages of development or transition among our cross-section of NDOs, because the study could not examine individual NDOs over time.[1] We also characterized NDOs according to 13 other variables such as staff size and level of community distress, to try to assure through such proxies a diversity in factors that might affect success. The selection process is described in more detail elsewhere.[2] The 12 NDOs studied are listed in Appendix B.

After choosing the sites, we collected and examined written materials on current and past NDO operations. We then visited each NDO for a period of four days. About 20 interviews were held at each site with NDO executive directors;[3] other key staff; board chairpersons and members; and relevant outsiders including funding sources, providers of technical assistance, political actors, and leaders of other community organizations.[4] The set of interview types and guides to questioning for each are detailed in "Field Work Design for Neighborhood Development Organizations Research."[5]

Two basic methodological approaches were taken both to collect information and to draw study conclusions. The first was direct. We asked NDO participants to identify the characteristics they thought were key to project success, the way those characteristics developed, and the usefulness of outside aid. We then identified consensus views and important differences across interviewees and sites. The second approach involved more inference

---

1. The study did call on NDO participants to describe the histories of their organizations but could not observe them directly.

2. "Identification of Sample Self-Help Neighborhood Development Organizations," Urban Institute Memorandum, May 1979.

3. Or heads of staff by other titles.

4. Or on occasion with key outsiders located in other places.

5. Urban Institute Memorandum, July 1979.

by the researchers. We collected information on how NDOs stood in terms of potentially key characteristics over time and on the project and capacity-building successes and failures they had experienced. We then drew our own conclusions across sites about the way observed factors influenced the observed outcomes. The findings reported are the results of the two approaches combined.

This paper was written entirely in terms of findings produced from experience at the 12 sites combined. We promised NDOs anonymity and therefore do not present separate case studies. The paper includes many examples in support of study conclusions but without attribution to individual NDOs.

Study findings are necessarily not completely definitive. Twelve NDOs cannot represent all the important variations in NDO experience. And when we examined particular phenomena, such as the special difficulties of larger, more experienced organizations or the usefulness of a specific type of outside aid, the relevant sample is even smaller. Also, all of the sample NDOs currently exist and are at least modestly successful. Factors that proved critical to the demise or stagnation of other neighborhood organizations may not be adequately observed. In addition, the study's measures of project success, upon which many inferences are based, are not precise. They consist more of site interviewees' descriptions of success and failure than of precise measurement. Neither study objectives nor resources provided for us to make detail direct measurement of the many project outcomes, over NDOs' entire histories, that helped form the basis for this research. And, as mentioned earlier, we had no opportunity actually to observe over time the development of individual NDOs.

Nonetheless, the study should add in a credible way to our store of knowledge about NDO growth and success in neighborhood revitalization efforts. Its base in intensive interviewing at multiple sites, focusing on special issues of project delivery and capacity building, is substantial in relation to previous efforts in this field. And this study is built carefully and deliberately on the previous work and accumulated expertise available on these subjects. Indeed, the study reports many findings that are consistent with the prior thinking of people directly involved in working with NDOs. The paper extends that knowledge, we believe, through careful empirical documentation; systematic presentation of a wide range of related observations and the links between them; increased specificity about the nature and impacts of NDO key characteristics, growth processes, and outside assistance; and the addition of new insights within each of the study objectives.

# APPENDIX B

## Sample NDOs

The following 12 neighborhood development organizations constitute our study sample. Their combined experiences in neighborhood revitalization activities serve as the primary source of information for this study.

| *Neighborhood Development Organization* | *Chief Administrator** |
|---|---|
| The Brightwood Corporation<br>200 Birnie Avenue<br>Springfield, Massachusetts | Austin Miller,<br>Executive Director |
| Chicanos Por La Causa<br>2333 East University Drive<br>Phoenix, Arizona | Tom Espinoza,<br>President/Executive Director |
| Chinatown Neighborhood Improvement<br>Resource Center<br>615 Grant Avenue<br>San Francisco, California | Gordon Chin,<br>Executive Director |
| Evanston Community Development<br>Corporation<br>1817 Church Street<br>Evanston, Illinois | Ernestine Jackson,<br>Executive Director |
| Jeff-Vander-Lou, Inc.<br>2953 Martin Luther King Drive<br>St. Louis, Missouri | Macler Shepard,<br>President |
| Los Sures (Southside United Housing<br>Development Fund, Inc.)<br>255 South 2nd Street<br>Brooklyn, New York 11211 | Wilfredo Vargas,<br>Administrator |
| Michigan Avenue Community<br>Organization<br>4330 Central<br>Detroit, Michigan | Ed Bobinchak,<br>Director |

*At time of study

| *Neighborhood Development Organization* | *Chief Administrator\** |
|---|---|
| Mississippi Action for Community<br>    Education<br>815 Main Street<br>Greenville, Mississippi | Charles Bannerman,<br>President/Executive Director |
| Operation Life<br>400 West Jackson<br>Las Vegas, Nevada | Ruby Duncan,<br>Executive Director |
| The Patch, Inc.<br>224 Carroll Street, S.E.<br>Atlanta, Georgia | Esther Lefever,<br>Executive Director |
| River East Economic Revitalization<br>    Corporation<br>222 Main Street<br>Toledo, Ohio | Don Monroe,<br>Administrator |
| Voice of the People<br>4927 North Kenmore<br>Chicago, Illinois | Barbara Beck<br>Development Coordinator |